1/68

BK 809.2 F932B
BERNARD SHAW AND THE THEATER IN THE NINETIES
/FROMM, HAR
1967 .00 M

3000 140804 40017
St. Louis Community College

809.2 F932b M
FROMM
BERNARD SHAW AND THE THEATER IN
THE NINETIES
5.00

D1173893

JUNIOR COLLEGE DISTRICT
of St. Louis - St. Louis County
LIBRARY
7508 Forsyth Blvd.
St. Louis, Missouri 63105

PRINTED IN U.S.A.

Bernard
SHAW
and the
THEATER
in the
NINETIES

A Study of Shaw's Dramatic Criticism

by Harold
FROMM

The University of Kansas
Lawrence
1967

© Copyright 1967 by the University of Kansas Press

Library of Congress Catalog Card Number: 67-14430

Printed in the U.S.A.

FOR MY
MOTHER and FATHER

PREFACE

BERNARD SHAW AND THE THEATER IN THE NINETIES is a study of the role Shaw played in English drama during the years he was a dramatic critic for the *Saturday Review*. Since the principles and standards which Shaw believed in during the nineties were those he was to maintain throughout his lifetime, his career as a dramatic critic is the very seed from which everything that is characteristically Shavian has emerged. Indeed, the statements Shaw made during this period were more detailed, vigorous, and fully developed than his later statements on the same subjects, because he evidently tired of repeating elaborate expositions.

At the risk of appearing to be a scholar who has become a bit unhinged as a result of too much seclusion, I would like to think that readers other than my confreres may find this book of interest. There are now a good many very specialized treatments of Shaw's opinions on dramatic theory and related subjects, mostly in unpublished dissertations, but there is no general account of Shaw's role in the theater of the nineties, dealing with his practical life, the censorship, the actors, the plays, and the prevailing views on Shakespeare and Ibsen. I have tried to provide such a treatment. The more specialized studies remain for those who wish to consult them, and I refer to them where relevant. And may I praise, as of quite special quality and interest, Eric Bentley's unique book on Shaw? Now that the anti-Shaw reaction is petering out, Shaw's genius, not as a supposed propagandist, but as an artist, begins to be viewed *sub specie aeternitatis,* if there is such a thing.

Thanks are given to Prof. Alvin Whitley of the University of Wisconsin, to Prof. Arthur Nethercot of Northwestern University, to the staff of the University of Kansas Press, to Marian Wilson for her several preparations of my manuscript, to Wayne State University for financial assistance, and to The Public Trustee and The Society of Authors for permission to quote copyright material from Shaw.

H. F.

August, 1966
Rochester, Michigan

CONTENTS

Chapter 1

SHAW THE DRAMATIC CRITIC

IN 1876, WHEN he was only twenty years old and a newcomer to London, Shaw began his career in criticism, fittingly enough, as a music critic for a weekly publication called the *Hornet*.[1] This position, if the role of ghost writer can be regarded as a position, was bestowed upon him by George John Vandeleur Lee, an old musical friend of Shaw's mother.[2] Shaw was cramming for a civil service job, when one day Lee offered him his own salary if he would review concerts for him. "I threw up my studies," Shaw later wrote, "and set to work to reform the musical profession. At the end of a year my friend was one of the most unpopular men in London, the paper was getting into difficulties, and complications were arising from the proprietor's doubts as to a critic who was not only very severe, but capable of being in two places at the same time. I gave that up too (making a virtue of necessity), and the proprietor presently retired, ruined."[3] I have called it fitting that Shaw began as a critic of music, for the critical and creative energy one finds in his writings can be traced back to the thoroughgoing effects of his musical childhood on his esthetic sensibility. Throughout his reviews of

1

drama and in his own plays we find implicit and explicit musical references of a kind indicating that a musical sensibility shaped most of his judgments of creative works as well as his plays.

The *Hornet* ceased publication the year after Shaw began to write his reviews, a fact which he immodestly attributed to himself, and not until 1885 did he begin to review once more, this time books for the *Pall Mall Gazette*. In June of 1880, however, Shaw sent several reviews to John Morley, editor of the *Gazette*, accompanied by a letter asking him whether they showed any promise. One of these pieces was a paper on *The Merchant of Venice*. "I should prefer writing on theatrical or musical events to manufacturing random articles, which is to me much the same thing as making bricks without straw."[4] Morley's reply is ironic, to say the least: "With regard to the question that you ask me, I cannot hesitate to say, that in my opinion you would do well to get out of journalism. It is a most precarious, dependent, and unsatisfactory profession, excepting for a very few who happen to have the knack, or manage to persuade people that they have it. . . . I wish I could have been of more service to you."[5]

The reviews which Shaw ultimately did write for the *Pall Mall Gazette* followed his famous meeting with William Archer in 1883, which Archer himself described in the *World* in 1892:

I used to be a daily frequenter of the British Museum Reading Room. Even more assiduous in his attendance was a young man of tawny complexion and attire, beside whom I used frequently to find myself seated. My curiosity was piqued by the odd conjunction of his subjects of research. Day after day for weeks he had before him two books, which he studied alternately, if not

simultaneously—Karl Marx's Das Kapital (in French),
and an orchestral score of Tristan und Isolde. I did not
know then how exactly this quaint juxtaposition sym-
bolised the main interests of his life. Presently I met
him at the house of a common acquaintance, and we
conversed for the first time. (*Prefaces*, p. 699)

Archer gave Shaw some books to review for the *Gazette*, which were followed by more, until reviews in
other journals, such as *Today*, *Our Corner*, the *Dramatic Review*, and the *Magazine of Music*, caused him
to neglect his contributions to the *Gazette*. In 1886
Archer was asked by Edmund Yates, editor of the
World, if he would take the place of his art critic, who
had died recently. "Encouraged by Shaw, he accepted,
on condition that Shaw went with him to the exhibi-
tions. When he received his first money, he sent Shaw
half, which Shaw returned. Archer sent it again and
Shaw again refused. . . . On this, Archer told the editor
. . . that the work was really being done by Shaw and
the latter was made art critic at fourpence a line. This
brought him rather less than £40 a year, but at the
same time he was being paid for art criticisms in *Our
Corner*."[6] Shaw wrote Archer in 1885: "Your mind is
in a thoroughly morbid condition with regard to the
pictures. I return the cheque, and recommend more
exercise and earlier hours. My moral ground is this. If
you are a competent critic, you do not need my assistance. If you are not competent, you are imposing on
Yates, and I cannot share the proceeds of a fraud. This,
I hope, is conclusive. If it is not, I can easily find a
fresh position equally elevated and inexpugnable."[7] In
1888 Shaw began to write music reviews again, now for
T. P. O'Connor, founder of the *Star*. He played the
role of Corno di Bassetto (his pseudonym as critic—

3

Italian for basset horn, a tenor clarinet in F) until 1890, complaining to O'Connor, "I am damned if I will go on after this month for two guineas. You know as well as I do that work at once so conscientious & brilliant cannot be kept up at such rates,"[8] whereupon he joined the *World* again, this time as music critic. His role as an art critic had ended as a result of his refusal to please the proprietress of the *World* by writing favorable notices—"puffs," as he called them—of the pictures painted by her friends. Shaw writes that her requests "were made in perfect good faith and all innocence, it never having occurred to those responsible that art criticism was a serious pursuit or that any question of morals or conduct could possibly arise over it. Of course, I resigned with some vigor, although without any ill-humor."[9] Shaw also resigned, in 1890, as art critic for *Truth*, because the editor wanted him to praise paintings he despised, and in 1891 he resigned from the *Observer* for similar reasons. In a letter, he wrote, "Truth is quarreling with me because I dont admire Goodall!!! My connection with the paper may not survive the language I have used in consequence."[10]

As music critic for the *World* Shaw first appeared to his audience as G.B.S. The *World* criticisms, along with those from the *Star*, were later collected into *London Music, 1888-89* and *Music in London*. However, in 1891 Shaw did not think enough of the *Star* articles to allow T. Fisher Unwin to publish them in book form. ". . . most of it is wretched stuff: in the few strips I have looked over there are not two paragraphs that I would reprint. . . . I think we had better leave di Bassetto to rot peacefully in his grave."[11] Happily, Shaw changed his mind and these volumes, together with the articles collected in *How to Become a Musical*

Critic,[12] reveal what has many times been called the best musical criticism ever written. They are as remarkable in their consistent quality, their wit, and their *avant garde* sensibility as the reviews of the drama. Indeed, Shaw did for music what he was later to do for drama: he helped to develop an audience for new genius, in this case Wagner, and he helped to restore authenticity in the performance of old music—Bach and Handel, for example—just as he was to do something comparable for Ibsen and Shakespeare a few years later.

That Shaw should have been a defender of Wagner was to be expected, for Wagner, both in his librettos and in his music, was an embodiment of the philosophy of Schopenhauer; even if Wagner misunderstood Schopenhauer enough to idealize love in *Tristan* by glorifying the Will to Live, he unconsciously illustrated Schopenhauer's observation that music, unlike the other arts, was not imitative but the thing-in-itself. Wagner had created a musical microcosm of his own, one which raised music above mere entertainment (this Brahms and Schumann, according to Shaw, were unable to do) to the level at which asceticism, mysticism, and ecstasy —in a word, the complete fulfillment of the human psyche—take place. What Wagner attempted to do in his way, Shaw was attempting to do in his, as critic, dramatist, and social reformer. How inevitable it was that Shaw should have been sympathetic to a musical counterpart of himself will be made clear in a subsequent chapter. But for the moment, one may observe that before Shaw became the champion of Ibsen, he was the champion of Wagner.

What is even more striking to a reader of our own day is that Shaw was aware of the violence being done

at the end of the nineteenth century to the music of
Bach and Handel, just as he was aware of the desecrations and distortions which were offered up in the name
of Shakespeare. After all, it was not until well into the
twentieth century, particularly the thirties and forties,
that reforms in the performance of Bach and Shakespeare began to be widespread, though Landowska's
Bach and Granville Barker's Shakespeare were pioneer-
ing ventures early in the century. Shaw's keen musical
sensibility detected at once what was wrong with Victorian re-creations of Bach and Handel: the incisive
rhythms, especially with the aid of soggy organ con-
tinuos, gradually were dissipated into plodding ambles,
made worse by choruses of preposterous dimensions—
three thousand for *Messiah*. Shaw also observed how
ill-suited was the timbre of the piano for performances
of Bach, and he knew how much better the music
sounded when played with the reedy and nasal old
harpsichords, woodwinds, and trumpets for which the
music was written.[13] Finally, Shaw saw through the
respectable piety of his day and believed, as Bach and
Handel believed, that piety and dreariness were not
inseparable and that church music should be no less
lively and invigorating than any other music. What is
more spirited than Bach's death arias? (Later, as a dramatic critic, Shaw ridiculed the presentations of Shakespeare's plays as virtually sacred—and dull—offerings.)
The young men and women of the choruses of the
nineties put up with a good deal of harsh criticism
from Shaw, but he was usually right and the musicolo-
gists of our own day support his views.

Shaw made it his conscious business to avoid technical jargon in his reviews of concerts, though he occasionally tossed off a paragraph of blazing unintelligi-

bility, just to prove to the exalted doctors of music that he could be as impressive in gibberish as they. He constantly criticized those who believed that form should be the chief concern of music, whether as a preoccupation on the part of a composer who was unable to communicate emotion, or a preoccupation with virtuoso brilliance on the part of a performer who could not play with feeling. He was hard, also, on performers who displayed themselves instead of doing justice to the music. That Shavian spirit which was later to appear as a violent denunciation of Barrymore's tamperings with *Hamlet* appears in the musical criticism as a mocking of Paderewski's athletic performances at the pianoforte.

The music criticism provides a good deal of insight into Shaw's esthetic criteria in general, especially in the great essay, "The Religion of the Pianoforte,"[14] and it even contains a good many passing remarks on the drama, the theater, and the actors, though most of what he says here is restated more fully and brilliantly in the dramatic reviews.

The lessons to be derived from the musical and dramatic reviews are similar: there is no substitute for taste and judgment—and above all, sensibility—when it comes to matters of art. The brilliance of the reviews is their consistent rightness, except for a few stubborn spots, which are the stains of mortality—a rightness which surely indicates the possession of faculties which are more delicate and perceptive than those of the majority of one's contemporaries. The obsolescent view of Shaw as a wild bull of rationalistic insensibility is rather absurd to anyone who has read his remarks about the arts. True, he did have blind spots. His antipathy against Brahms is hard to understand now (the Wagner-Brahms opposition of the nineteenth century seems

7

alien and strange to us), and his constant and immoderate dislike of Brahms's *A German Requiem* is bizarre. But these are trifles when set against the whole picture.

In 1894, after four years of incessant attendance at concerts, Shaw made up his mind "to take the opportunity of Edmund Yates's death to escape from musical criticism, which is not so amusing to the writer who has written a long article on the subject for seven years as it is to his readers."[15] He wrote a letter to Arthur Griffiths, who succeeded Yates, to explain why he would not continue to write about music for the *World*: "Yates's selection of us [Shaw, Archer, and Theodore Childs] shewed that whether he was fully conscious or not, he could be depended on to feel his way in the right direction; and also that his instinct included an appreciation of the backing of real character which is necessary to save an unconventional paper from lapsing into blackguardism. . . . you are likely to reverse Yates's policy & proceed on the assumption that society likes the sort of loyal, constitutional, jingo, pietistic slosh it has to pretend to like."[16] He then went on to explain that he was getting tired and uninspired, that he would want more money, and that Griffiths could hire a fresher, younger man for less. The escape from musical criticism was followed by the more than three years of dramatic reviews which form the bulk of *Our Theatres in the Nineties*, criticisms contributed weekly to the *Saturday Review*, from January 1895 to May 1898. The escape, however, was never really complete, for the basis of a good deal of Shaw's criticism of the drama is the musical sensibility which produced music reviews of such distinction during those earlier years.

Shaw's position as dramatic critic for the *Saturday*

Review is discussed by Frank Harris in his book on Shaw:

In the early nineties I bought the *Saturday Review* and changed it from a Conservative weekly living on a reputation which it had survived to something alive which still haunts London on the reputation I renewed for it. I knew that Shaw was exhausted as a music critic and could now only repeat himself—he admitted as much—and anyhow I did not want Yates's leavings. When he had done a review or two for me I proposed that he should do a weekly theatre feuilleton for the *Saturday*.

He made two conditions. First, the paper must break with its tradition of anonymity and the old-fashioned "we," and print his articles in the first person over the now familiar signature G.B.S. Agreed. Second, six pounds a week. Agreed.

Of course he made good. It was the peak of his achievement as a journalist, and his last regular job in that profession.[17]

Shaw at first refused the job, in November 1894, recommending instead Golding Bright, the young critic of *Advice to a Young Critic*, but Harris pressed him until he eventually accepted in 1895.

Several years earlier, in a letter, Shaw had expressed in great detail his reasons for preferring signed articles:

I have not profoundly considered the subject of signed articles; but I am, roughly & practically speaking, in favor of signatures, because, though I am the most conscientious of men, I write more carefully, and with a keener sense of direct personal responsibility for the soundness of my utterances, when what I write appears over my signature. Furthermore, I write with greater freedom when I bear the whole responsibility myself.

9

Again, I like to get credit for my own brilliancy, because this secures to me personally the full "rent" of my ability, whereas, when I write anonymously, it is absorbed by the newspaper proprietor.[18]

Shaw was motivated to become dramatic critic for the *Saturday Review* by his reluctance to depend on his plays for a living. The plays he had written by this time, unfortunately, were receiving little attention, with the exception of *Arms and the Man*, which had a stage success. *Widowers' Houses* had been performed in 1892. That was about the extent of the performances of his plays. As a result, he felt that reviewing would offer a regular income and some measure of financial security, as proved to be correct, although he did not earn enough to be able to accumulate any savings. But, as it turned out, his financial status improved considerably through the American success of *Arms and the Man*, from which he obtained substantial royalties. He wrote to William Archer, just before he began as critic for the *Saturday Review*: "My extreme reluctance to make myself dependent for my bread and butter on the acceptance of my plays by managers tempts me to hold to the position that my real profession is that by which I can earn my bread in security. Anyhow, I am prepared to do anything which will enable me to keep my plays for twenty years with perfect tranquillity if it takes that time to educate the public into wanting them."[19]

It is pleasant to read what Shaw had to say many years later about his own dramatic criticism, because his early prophecies are seen to have been based on a good assessment of his abilities. In 1896, while he was still in the midst of his reviewing, he wrote: "Some day they will reprint my articles; and then what will all your puffs and long runs and photographs and papered houses and cheap successes avail you, O lovely leading ladies and well-tailored actor-managers? The twentieth century, if it concerns itself about either of us, will see you as I see you" (II, 160-161). And after his career as reviewer had ended, he looked back on his reviews as "weekly columns, which I once filled full from a magic well that never ran dry or lost its sparkle provided I pumped hard enough" (*Prefaces*, p. 717). And still later, at the age of ninety-two, he wrote: "My weekly feuilletons on all the fine arts in succession are still readable after sixty years" (*Self-Sketches*, p. 116).

It is no secret that Shaw's egotistical method was a calculated literary tactic, but if any doubt should remain, Shaw himself discusses his method many times. He compares himself to George Henry Lewes, for example, "in his free use of vulgarity and impudence whenever they happened to be the proper tools for his job" (II, 161), and elsewhere reveals that "in this world if you do not say a thing in an irritating way, you may just as well not say it at all, since nobody will trouble themselves about anything that does not trouble them" (II, 85-86). Added to this shock treatment was Shaw's Joey-the-Clown pose (to use Mrs. Campbell's name for him): "Iconoclasms, seditions, and blasphemies, if well turned, tickle those whom they shock; so that the critic adds the privileges of the court jester to those of the confessor" (*Prefaces*, p. 717). After a while, however, his audience became unable to take him seriously at some of his most serious moments. "All I had to do was to open my normal eyes . . . to be applauded as the most humorously extravagant paradoxer in London" (*Prefaces*, p. 717). Why can't you be serious? they kept asking him, when actually he was serious all the time.

Shaw, of course, prided himself on his honesty and lack of gentlemanliness, for though gentlemanliness, he believed, is bad enough in itself, in a critic it is indefensible. Critical truthfulness and gentlemanliness do not go together. "I doubt if it was ever worth being a gentleman" (III, 74), he said, and he then condemned that "amiable and shameless friendliness which gradually and inevitably mollifies criticism in London" (III, 151). There are two splendid examples of Shaw's conscientious lack of amiability as a critic which are worth mentioning. Shaw had always spoken harshly of the conductor, Augustus Harris, during his life, and when, after his death, the papers published the usual deferential résumés of the deceased's achievements, Shaw merely repeated what he had said of Harris while he was alive, concluding: "I said it all when he was alive; I say it now that he is dead; and I shall say it again whenever I see the Press bowing a little too low before commercial success, and offering it the wreaths that belong to genius and devotion alone" (II, 180).

The other example is Shaw's reply to Ellen Terry when she told him that she did not like being discussed in reviews: "As to not mentioning you in public, I understand the feeling: but I am not convinced. Before the world I must deal sincerely with you, however light a turn I may give my sincerity. I owe that to your dignity as an artist and to my profession."[20]

Shaw's egotistical method and his bluntness are essential aspects of his prose style. That style, so effortless, forceful, and, when necessary, devastating, has been examined carefully at least twice—years ago by Dixon Scott, recently and more exhaustively by Richard Ohmann.[21] In "The Innocence of Bernard Shaw," Scott praises the Shavian mode as "the very finest example in the whole range of English letters of prose written to be uttered with physical forcibleness on the rapid levels of man-to-man speech, and yet retaining, unsuspected, all those subtle powers of balance, of rhythm and picturesqueness, whose aid must be employed before all defenses can be carried and which steal triumphantly into the citadel of the mind of the hearer through insidious emotional doorways whilst the colloquialisms keep the common sense engaged."[22] Yet Scott finds that Shaw has been hoist with his own petard: "The parallel-bars of his prose have seemed to us thus far a firm apparatus on which he could perform acrobatically. We have now to face the fact that they were the bars of a cage, and that Shaw had shut himself and his capers inside it. . . . The aesthetic fashion of the hour favoured contempt, tirades, antagonisms, an omniscient schoolmastering of creation. Instead of wearing it a moment and then tossing it aside, this man hugged it to him till it became a second skin."[23] Scott here raises the relevant esthetic question: To what extent does style shape the thought, to what extent are style and thought the same? Perhaps Scott regards Shaw's style as too distinguishable from his ideas to suit post New-Critical readers, who are prone to see a tighter relationship between the two. The variety of styles that Shaw could employ in his various fictional works would seem to weaken the view that Shaw was involuntarily limited by too few strings on his lute. Shaw could be charming, coy, titillating—not merely schoolmasterly, yet Scott's observations are illuminating as far as they go. (Ohmann's more thorough analysis is too specialized to deal with here.) At any rate, the polemical mode that Scott finds so pervasive in Shaw is characteristic of his criticism of the arts and is pronounced in the reviews of the drama.

Shaw realized that the obstacles to good criticism were many and that to maintain critical integrity required what almost amounted to cruelty. He had many times to fight off people who saw no reason why he could not write favorable reviews when they asked him to do so, and he criticized other reviewers who were less able to resist the implications of complimentary tickets. "To try to prevent me from criticizing by pointing out to me the superior pecuniary advantages of puffing is like trying to keep a young Irving from going on the stage by pointing out the superior pecuniary advantages of stockbroking" (I, 247). He relates, in the review of April 13, 1895, how conscience forced him to resign two "very desirable positions on the critical staff of London papers of first-rate pretension—in one case because I was called upon . . . to write corrupt puffs of the editor's personal friends, with full liberty, in return, to corruptly puff my own; and in the other, because my sense of style revolted against the interpolation in my articles of sentences written by the proprietor's wife to express her high opinion of artists, unknown to fame and me, who had won her heart by their hospitality" (I, 88). In the appendix to *The Quintessence of Ibsenism* a long discussion of the forces which prevent good dramatic criticism from springing up—the editors' lack of interest in art, the corruptibility of the run-of-the-mill critic, the fear of incurring libel suits by criticizing notables—concludes:

All this does not mean that the entire Press is hopelessly corrupt in its criticism of Art. But it certainly does mean that the odds against the independence of the Press critic are so heavy that no man can maintain it completely without a force of character and a personal authority which are rare in any profession, and which in most of them can command higher pecuniary terms and prospects than any which journalism can offer. . . . I do not exaggerate or go beyond the warrant of my own experience when I say that unless a critic is prepared not only to do much more work than the public will pay him for, but to risk his livelihood every time he strikes a serious blow at the powerful interests vested in artistic abuses of all kinds (conditions which in the long run tire out the strongest man), he must submit to compromises which detract very considerably from the trustworthiness of his criticism.[24]

Elsewhere, Shaw writes: "These unhappy men [the critics] will write you up or write you down, as the case may be, in the newspapers; but they are pretty sure to write you up, because in writing you down they have to be extremely careful what they say lest you should have the law of them, whereas in paying you compliments they may say what they please without the least anxiety to themselves or their editors" (III, 184).

When Shaw resigned as art critic for the Observer, he enumerated the kinds of violence which were performed upon his work:

Just a hasty line to explain the row about the Observer. Cooke is such an unspeakable greenhorn that when he got my article—which I need hardly say was a very good one—he could not make head or tail of it. So instead of sending to me, he helplessly handed it to his "proprietor," who proceeded to mutilate it, interpolate scraps of insufferable private view smalltalk, break it into paragraphs in the wrong places, season it with obvious little puffs of his private friends, and generally reduce its commercial value (not to speak of its artistic value) about 1800%. If you look at the article, you will see at a glance the broken fragments of Shaw sticking ridiculously in the proprietary mud. You can imagine my feelings on seeing good work spoiled in this fashion by a couple of duffers. . . .[25]

But the question of critical truthfulness is not as simple as it appears. Shaw pointed out to William Archer that even the most scrupulous critic—Archer himself, for example—unconsciously represses and alters his criticism to avoid offense which might ultimately harm his own wife and children. Shaw, whose family ties were not as demanding as Archer's, could risk penury more readily than many other critics. "You know," he wrote Archer, "that I lost about £100 a year for refusing to criticise in the private interests of Mrs Labouchere [wife of the proprietor of *Truth*]. Do you doubt that Mrs Labouchere interferes in the dramatic criticism as well, considering her past?" Then he adds, "But compare my Fabian Essays and my Quintessence with my World articles, bold as the last affect to be; and you will find the butter on my mother's bread and my own sticking to my fingers. What would my writing be if I had a wife and family, and had no more ability than any of the men who are craving for my berth today? This is not Stupidity: it is Poverty and Servitude. I prostitute myself as honestly as I can; but I am bought and sold for all that."[26] "But it is one thing to say that the critic is not to blame for making certain concessions: it is quite another to assert that the concessions are not made, or to infer that because they dont matter individually they dont matter socially."[27] This is an astute and characteristically candid

16

consideration. Its ultimate ramifications for criticism are important, for the unconscious pressures of society upon public statements shape such statements more than we are aware, especially those of critics whose judgments are unsteady and uncertain. Encouragingly, a comparison of Shaw's public and private statements, as they appear in the published criticism and correspondence, reveals that as far as he was aware he usually said what he felt and meant.

Although Shaw wrote with the utmost candor, he made a great effort to detect inhumanity and purge it from his reviews, in order to avoid giving needless pain. "Those who think the things I say severe, or even malicious, should just see the things I do not say" (I, 247). But, he adds, no matter how much he may soften his words, he is more or less incorruptible.

During his reviewing days, Shaw struck up a friendship with the aspiring critic Golding Bright, after a performance of Arms and the Man. When Shaw came onstage after the play to address the audience, there was a solitary boo. The booer, who turned out to be Bright, received a quick-witted reply: "My dear fellow," Shaw called up to him, "I quite agree with you; but what are we two against so many?"[28] Characteristically, Shaw became a good friend of the booer and went out of his way to help him in his career, giving him all sorts of journalistic scoops to develop in his own reviews in the Sun. What is more, Shaw wrote interviews with himself which he sent to Bright for his column, enabling him to have exclusive (and controlled) interviews with the eminent G.B.S. He also gave Bright advice based on his own experience and success, told him to study the drama in the reading room of the British Museum, where he could enjoy without charge the advantages of electric light, ink, and paper, and advised him to write a thousand words every day and some long books as practice, to read Lamb, Wagner, and Hazlitt, and to go to orchestral concerts, theaters, debating societies, and political meetings—in a word, to be a young Shaw.[29] His specific instructions on the art of writing reviews provide insight into Shaw's own work. When Bright reviewed Shaw's *Plays Pleasant and Unpleasant* unfavorably, Shaw wrote him: "Further, you pitched into an author without offending him, a thing that can only be done by saying your mind quite sincerely."[30] But when Bright was very harsh to a young actor, Shaw wrote: "If you want to enjoy masterly acting twenty years hence, you must be very tender to the apprentices and journeymen of to-day."[31] As to criticism of writers of plays, Shaw told him:

You must give up detesting everything appertaining to Oscar Wilde or to anyone else. The critic's first duty is to admit, with absolute respect, the right of every man to his own style. . . . There is always a vulgar cry both for and against every man or woman of any distinction; and from such cries you cannot keep your mind too clear if you wish to attain distinction yourself. . . . Excuse this scrap of sermon: I would not intrude it upon you if I did not know by experience the great difficulty of forming and holding to a genuine original opinion of public men on their own merits when so many fools are chattering about them in all directions.[32]

Among these letters is one which contains Shaw's annotation of Bright's review of Sardou's *Odette*:
"Bright: . . . but under no circumstances can it be called a great play.

"Shaw: It does not pretend to be a great play. The remark is equally true of Box and Cox, which is nevertheless a very good farce. The question is, is Odette a good play *of its class*, and what you mean is that it isn't."[33]

At the same time, Shaw tried to encourage Bright by telling him that in London all beginners were forty, with twenty years of obscure hard work behind them, twenty years which were by no means the worst part of their lives. Here again Shaw had himself in mind.[34]

We can see from these letters that Shaw was at heart a remarkably kind man whose apparent maliciousness was merely the rhetoric of his moral-esthetic. He once told Mrs. Campbell: "In all these years I have hurt many people as the Doctor hurt your thumb, sometimes sorely perhaps, but never maliciously, never desiring to hurt, never without such anodynes as my wit and address could devise. I have never said anything false or unjust or spiteful, and never wanted to."[35] In one of his dramatic reviews, Shaw relates how he cried at a performance of *Olivia*, an adaptation of *The Vicar of Wakefield*, and in a letter to Ellen Terry he writes: "Yet you brought tears to my eyes, not, you will understand, by the imaginary sorrows of the lunatic (sorrow does not make me cry, even when it is real) but by doing the thing beautifully. My whole claim to be a critic of art is that I can be touched in that way."[36] What is interesting here is that Shaw's delicate sensibility did not incline him toward sentimentality but rather made him, the remarks of Chesterton to the contrary, well suited to make esthetic judgments of a high order. One need only compare a review by Shaw with one by Clement Scott or William Archer to see how disinterested and esthetic Shaw's judgment could be, for all his moral fervor.

Shaw did not think very highly of most of his fellow dramatic critics, and he was as much at pains to instruct *them* by means of his reviews as to inform his audience:

My real aim is to widen the horizon of the critic, especially of the dramatic critic, whose habit at present is to bring a large experience of stage life to bear on a scanty experience of real life, although it is certain that all really fruitful criticism of the drama must bring a wide and practical knowledge of real life to bear on the stage. . . . our dramatic critics specialize themselves to such an extent that they lose the character of men and citizens, and become mere playgoers, in which unhappy condition, since stageland then appears a quite real place to them, and the laws of Nature are supplanted in their minds by the conventions of the stage, every fresh permutation and combination of the old stage situations and effects appeals to them as a historical, evolutional development. They tell the story of Fedora and discuss her motives and character when there is really nothing whatever to discuss except how Sarah Bernhardt, or Mrs Bernard Beere, or Mrs Patrick Campbell make this or that effect. (I, 187-188)

Of the dramatic critics of his day, Shaw refers most frequently to Clement Scott and William Archer. In their critical methods, these men were different, neither Archer nor Scott being able to lay claim to the combination of vigor and penetrating intellect so characteristic of Shaw.

Clement Scott[37] was an extremely popular critic, with a large following, and he was an apt spokesman for middle-class morality, the very morality which Shaw spent most of his time trying to destroy. Scott became a dramatic critic in 1863 and wrote reviews for the *Sunday Times* for two years. In view of Shaw's later criticism of Scott, one is surprised to learn that Scott was forced to leave the paper because he was too outspoken. In 1870 he joined the *London Figaro* and in 1871 became dramatic critic for the *Daily Telegraph*, for which he wrote reviews until 1898, gaining great popularity. Scott had little concern with either esthetic or dramatic theory and was not accustomed to questioning conventional assumptions about the nature of drama or the art of acting. In fairness to him, it should be said that in his own best days he was a champion of the Robertsonian drama, itself a revolutionary movement, but by the time Shaw began to campaign for the counter-revolutionary drama of ideas, Scott was still a Robertsonian and thus a reactionary force. Indeed, he had not only embraced the drama of Robertson, he had written some plays of his own, including adaptations from the French of Sardou, another of Shaw's whipping boys. His major success was *Off the Line* (1871), an English version of Sardou produced by the Bancrofts, followed by *Peril* and *Diplomacy*, also from Sardou.

As to his character as a man, one writer has observed:

In short, in everything from his elegant moustaches to his attitude toward women, he was what we think of as the typical late-Victorian of middle class. Archer and Shaw, when read today, sound comparatively modern. . . . But Scott "bears a date," and reminds us of all those men of the Nineties who have figured in so many popular books of this generation—the type of Clarence Day's famous father, with his extroverted combativeness, his satisfaction with the *status quo*, and his energy. Scott was a practical, forceful, singleminded man, without much introspection, original intelligence, or profundity, but with remarkable fitness for the particular role he was to play.[38]

In the light of Scott's antipathy to Ibsen and to post-Robertsonian drama in general, Shaw is relatively kind to him before he destroys him:

> Mr Clement Scott is not the first of the great dramatic critics; but he is the first of the great dramatic reporters. Other men may have hurried from the theatre to the newspaper to prepare, red hot, a notice of the night's performance for the morning's paper; but nobody did it before him with the knowledge that the notice was awaited by a vast body of readers conscious of his personality and anxious to hear his opinion. . . .
>
> The main secret of Mr Scott's popularity is that he is above all a sympathetic critic. His susceptibility to the direct expression of human feeling is so strong that he can write with positive passion about an exhibition of it which elicits from his colleagues only some stale, weary compliment. . . . (II, 139)

Shaw goes on to say that Scott's criticism is distinguished for its warmth of personal feeling, but that it is personal feeling and nothing more. Scott, he continues, is insensible to art, is not capable of profound thought and, since he has nothing more than immediate feeling to go by, reacts unfavorably to anything new which excites unpleasant feelings in him. For all practical purposes, Shaw disqualifies him as a critic. As to his philistinism, Shaw remarks that "when Ibsen's *Ghosts* forced the old ideas to take up the challenge of the new, Mr Scott was the only critic whose attack on Ibsen was really memorable" (II, 142). What equivocation! Scott's fulminations against *Ghosts* became a *locus classicus* of philistinism, not only for Shaw but for virtually everyone who has written about nineteenth-century drama since. Lest Shaw's estimate of Scott seem prejudiced, Miriam Franc, in her book on Ibsen, observes: "Scott was sentimental, prejudiced, and reactionary. He saw in Ibsen a foe to decency and a reviler of sacred things, and he was sincerely shocked."[39] His notions of decency were apparently related to his Roman Catholicism, which Shaw alludes to in *The Quintessence of Ibsenism.*

William Archer and Shaw, on the other hand, were good friends who did not hesitate to insult each other in their reviews, Shaw writing a review mocking Archer and Archer retaliating with criticism of both Shaw and his mockeries.

Archer's background[40] included Protestant parents who belonged to two small separatist sects, the Walkerites and the Glasites, whose meetings they attended while they lived in Scotland. Archer's having relatives in Norway may account for his interest in Norwegian language and literature. After a brief apprenticeship on the *London Figaro,* where he reviewed the drama for two years, Archer wrote for the *World,* the *Nation,* the *Tribune,* the *Morning Leader,* and the *Manchester Guardian.* During these years as critic he was also translating the plays of Ibsen, and in 1880 his version of *Pillars of Society* marked the debut of Ibsen in London. Miriam Franc writes: "Of all the critics who supported Ibsen dramas in these trying times, Archer was the recognized leader. To quote Mr. Gosse: 'For a quarter of a century he was the protagonist in the fight against misconstruction and stupidity; with wonderful courage, with not less wonderful good temper and persistency, he insisted on making the true Ibsen take the place of the false, and in securing for him the recognition due to his genius.' "[41] Although Archer undertook this great labor of translation and was, naturally, an admirer of Ibsen, he lacked that intellectual ardor and passion so typical of Shaw. To Shaw, Archer was a man who cared for the theater as a source of make-believe and escape rather than as a pulpit, who was interested mainly in the semblance of reality which the stage tries to achieve (I, 91). Shaw admitted that Archer's reviews had classic restraint, unlike his own, which were the work of a demagogue and soapbox orator (III, 157), but Archer disapproved of the Shavian method and spoke against it very particularly in one of his reviews: "Now I venture to suggest that this machine gun style of criticism, mowing alike the stage and the auditorium, and leaving Mr. Shaw in sole and undivided possession of eyes, ears, brains, and capacity for Shakespeare, is not the highly skilled work we have a right to expect of him. . . . It flies to extreme and imaginary standards—to ideals of perfection non-existent within the critic's experience—in order to depress and crush earnest effort."[42] Furthermore, Archer believed that all that Shaw could see in Shakespeare was Shakespeare's lack of concern with nineteenth-century problems: "For my part, I have long ago given up as a bad job the attempt to convert Shakespeare to my 'views.' I have long ago ceased to look to the author of *Coriolanus* for an enlightened sympathy with democratic ideals, or to the adaptor of *The Taming of the Shrew* for advanced opinions on the woman question."[43] Whereas Shaw complained about Archer's Calvinistic seriousness (I, 250), Archer deplored Shaw's extravagant critical method and his interest in ideas. Yet for all Shaw's wildness and all Archer's caution and restraint, Archer was relatively obtuse about the quality of Pinero's work, to cite one example.[44]

Arthur Bingham Walkley,[45] another critic of Shaw's day, is remembered today principally as the dedicatee of *Man and Superman*. In the late seventies, Walkley began as a Post Office clerk and then had a series of civil service jobs while, at the same time, serving successively as dramatic critic for the *Star*, the *Speaker*, and *The Times*. He thought of himself as an impressionist who examined his own sensations about a work of art, eschewing rules. Art, according to his view, is primarily sensuous pleasure. Although at first he liked Ibsen, he developed an antipathy to the drama of ideas, especially as typified by Shaw, and in his later years he was less delighted by Ibsen than by conventional light comedies. Shaw caricatured him as Trotter in *Fanny's First Play*.

Shaw's criticism has a quality not found in that of his contemporaries, an organic and consistent view of drama, animated by a fiery personality with strong opinions. When one has a fine sensibility and extensive knowledge, nothing is more useful than strong opinions. Although other critics of Shaw's day had knowledge, like Archer, or emotions, like Scott, or sensibility, like Walkley, none of them had them all and in such felicitous admixture as Shaw. As one Shavian scholar has remarked: "As a critic of painting, of music, of the drama, what he was fighting for so violently was to vindicate the ways of the artist, his freedom and integrity, against the indifference and inertia of the Philistines."[46] This vindication will be illustrated in the chapters that follow.

Chapter 2

ETHICS, ESTHETICS, AND METAPHYSICS

It is fashionable to say that Shaw's main concerns were politics and sociology, but if these were his main concerns they were only as means rather than as ends. Shaw could never have been a thoroughgoing philosopher, because his thought was always impelled to transform itself into action. For him it was always necessary to take up those activities whereby ideals are made into realities. This is how he came to busy himself with the Fabians and soapbox oratory and sociological and meta-biological drama. And this is why we cannot discuss, sui generis, Shaw's dramatic theory. For the drama was to him merely one medium for establishing the Heavenly City on earth, a city of beauty, order, and morality —ultimately, as in Back to Methuselah, a realm of pure, disembodied Platonic Ideas. Although he thought he did not care for art for art's sake, he was an esthete like Matthew Arnold, like Ruskin, like Schopenhauer, like many other nineteenth-century thinkers whose main concern was with order and beauty and their application to daily life. Since art is the highest human embodiment of order and beauty, Shaw often raises the question, Why, then, do we thinkers and artists become social reformers? His reply is invariably the same: If we do not translate our vision of order and beauty into daily life, there is no one else to do it. And so, although he is originally concerned with beauty in art, like Ruskin he is carried further and further afield because each step in the right direction reveals more and more obstacles to be overcome. After a while art is almost obscured from sight, as politics and sociology seem to usurp every moment of time and every ounce of energy. But the original impetus remains—it is a desire to communicate a vision of beauty to the world and to make the world itself beautiful, especially by means of the order which results from love of the arts and from morality and ethics in daily life, not to mention sanitation and the elimination of poverty. But the higher life cannot be participated in until the lower elements of human nature are properly conditioned.

The major problem that must be faced before we can even begin to look at Shaw's understanding of the nature and function of art is the radical one which lies behind every critical study of Shaw's work: Is Shaw's character principally esthetic, sensuous, and passionate, or is it principally unesthetic, puritanical, and frigidly intellectual? Until only a few years ago, there was almost no criticism of Shaw by literary critics, although there has been a superabundance of biographical and historical examination of his career. Very likely, as Bruce R. Park has suggested,[1] Shaw's writings were regarded, not as literature, but as propaganda beneath serious consideration by literary critics. If one assumes that Shaw's personality is utterly unesthetic, one is left with a vast mass of writings consisting of a program of ideas that cannot be examined esthetically. Further-

28

more, if one makes such an assumption, Shaw's own value as a critic of the arts is reduced almost to nothing.]

The critics who read Shaw as a Platonic mystic ultimately come to the conclusion, though not always explicitly, that Shaw is seeking a kind of Nirvana, accessible only through ascent of the Platonic Ladder to the realm of pure Ideas and the consequent annihilation of self and personality. There is no place for art in such a world, except perhaps as a primary rocket used to get one off the ground and into orbit. After the ascent, art is no longer needed. For example, Ludwig Lewisohn, in "Shaw Among the Mystics," writes:

That magnificent intellect has always been a little disembodied. His asceticism is icy and his fastidiousness not quite human. He regards sex as a nuisance and art as a bauble. He is offended not only by disorder and dirt; he is offended by the processes of procreation and metabolism. In a word, he hates the body. . . . In no sense will mankind take his bleak parable [Back to Methuselah] to heart. It is the monument of a great despair. But men do not despair. They are sustained by the very things that Shaw holds to be negligible if not noxious—by love and art, food and wine, and even by a little warmth when, after darkness, the goodly sun returns.[2]

And Robert Brustein writes: "For Shaw is not simply dissatisfied with certain human activities; he sometimes seems to be in rebellion against the very nature of human existence. The bodiless character of Shaw's Superman—not to mention Shaw's own vegetarianism, teetotalism, and abstention from sexual intercourse after his marriage—indicates a kind of Swiftian disgust at the human body and its functions."[3] And in one of the most stimulating and provocative of all the books about Shaw, C. E. M. Joad writes: "Shaw's life has contained little of the emotional; scarcely anything of the sensuous. It has been almost entirely lacking in the sensations and the emotions that men have commonly derived from drink, from Nature and from sensual and emotional love. Shaw is, in fact, a Puritan. Therefore, he tends to find in music what men who live out more fully and variously to the full scope and range of their senses normally find in nature, in sexual relations, in the athletic pleasures of the body and the sensation of the palate."[4] And, of course, Chesterton's whole book is based on the view of Shaw as a fastidious and fanatical puritan who is too dried out to enjoy life by means of a vigorous Catholic romp.

This picture of Shaw as a totally unesthetic personality has appalling implications, for what can we do with his criticisms of Shakespeare, his defense of talky Ibsen plays, and his own creations, if we accept such an account? On the other hand, quite contrary descriptions of Shaw's personality are also available. Replying to a critic who underscored Shaw's puritanism, Dixon Scott remarked: " 'Austérité aigre et hargneuse' be hanged! The lad's life was a voluptuous revel. He dreamed and dawdled at school, where he was only a desultory dayboy . . . and at home, the less distracted, he simply soaked himself lusciously in the licensed orgies and ecstasies of music. Melody, grand opera melody, not only, for him, took the place of the prose of real life, he even dissolved all his books in it, making it a vehicle for absorbing Scott and Victor Hugo and Poe, in an absolutely sensuous physical form."[5] Eric Bentley writes: "The experience of Beauty in the arts—especially in music—was to Shaw tantamount to mystical experience of the divine."[6] Shaw himself has written about his experiences of the arts many times, and though he consciously stresses the ability of literature to teach, he also consistently reveals his emotional excitation: "You cannot read it as you do the paragraphs in The Times that contain mere accurate information; it acts on your senses and imagination in some strange way that, although you do not altogether understand the content of it, yet you feel that it is a great ringing message. . . . It startles you, and you take an extraordinary delight in it."[7] "I claim to be a voluptuary rather than an ascetic: I do without beefsteak because I hate it; but never deny myself a Beethoven symphony performance if I can help it."[8] "But ability does not become genius until it has risen to the point at which its keenest states of perception touch on ecstasy, on healthy, self-possessed ecstasy. . . ."[9] (Here he contrasts for Janet Achurch the exhilaration from art with the drugged high spirits produced by alcohol and sex, alcohol having been her addiction.) And, as a final illustration: "Now the effect the artist produces on others is that of unlimitedness; and it is this great mystery and infinitude which attracts us all to art at first in these days."[10]

Certainly, even from the few passages I have chosen to quote, it is necessary to admit that Shaw's ecstatic response to certain types of artistic experiences, and especially to musical ones, verges on the mystical and finally, in Back to Methuselah, enters a world of bald Platonic Ideas, divorced from the senses. Shaw himself has attacked the arts many times as, for example, when he writes in a letter: "If the dockhands came to me tomorrow and said that they were going to start burning and demolishing, but could not make up their minds what to start on, I should recommend them to go for the works of art first as for their most dangerous rivals in the attention of the thoughtful."[11] But here, as in most similar references to art, he is disapproving of art for art's sake estheticism in which art is a substitute for life instead of an *intensification* of it. Shaw's own love of art, as I have noted earlier, led him closer to society rather than further away from it, until he appeared to be completely enmeshed in social activities. Joad observes that as Shaw becomes more and more Platonic, he moves from the view that art is a window on reality to the view that art is a childish substitute for reality,[12] but this alteration in perspective takes place over a long period of years. In the early part of his life, and while he is still a critic, the sensuous elements of art have for him a much stronger self-justification than they do by 1920.

From the positions outlined above, we appear to be left either with two unreconcilable pictures of Shaw's personality—the ascetic versus the ecstatic—or a single picture of a man whose sensuous inclinations have all been channeled into the narrow streams of music and art, leaving an otherwise ascetic personality to cope with all the rest of life's experiences. I do not believe, however, that these views bequeath to us a Shaw who cannot write plays—only tracts—or who cannot write criticisms—only programs. In fact, we have seen these contradictions before—in Plato, in St. Augustine, in Edmund Spenser, and in John Milton, to name just a few eminent specimens. Let us, for the sake of convenience, call this phenomenon the Platonic Personality.

Some of the letters published recently for the first time add a new dimension to this picture of Shaw as a Platonic Personality. Of special interest are the details that are revealed about his mania for bicycle riding. Shaw took long cycling trips around the English countryside, instructed William Archer on how to buy a bike for his son, and repeatedly bashed himself up, sometimes seriously, in collisions with other bicycles as well as stationary objects. From a letter to Janet Achurch we can examine a typical Shavian bicycle experience.

The other evening, after riding over thirty miles up hill & down dale, and finishing by fifteen miles at full speed to escape being overtaken by darkness (I had left my lamp at home), I was so abominably tired after pushing the thing up the lane that when I mounted to try and ride a level bit, I tumbled off. I thought I was alighting on a grass strip by the way side; but it was a briar bush which let me gracefully down to the bottom of a deep ditch. The bicycle fell over me across the top of the ditch, and as I lay there looking up peacefully at the moon through the spokes of the wheel and the laced thorntwigs of the briar, I felt blessedly happy and at rest.[13]

Although this is one of the less violent of the cycling upsets revealed in the letters, it does not present us with a picture of a man lacking sexual energies, a sense of beauty, or a passionate personality. Indeed, speeding in automobiles, racing on bicycles, and a repeated practice of getting into violent and dangerous accidents are often regarded as expressions of primary sexual energy. The impression we get of Shaw during the first half of his life is of a man who, while not particularly enthusiastic about direct sexual activity, was addicted to compulsive and often self-destructive bicycle riding and passionate and nervously excited music. And no matter how ascetic he may appear in his other

33

guises, we cannot fail to keep this side of his nature always present in our examinations of his life and works. What causes Shaw's personality ultimately to seem religious and at least semi-mystical to us is the dissatisfaction he constantly reveals in connection with short-term sensuous and appetitive satisfactions. The great "puritans" and spiritual-religious figures in our heritage are invariably the most passionate and insatiable. Plato's ladder of love was designed to lead from brief, and therefore frustrating, sexual experiences, to one protracted satisfaction, which becomes indistinguishable from absence of desire. Augustine turned from the life of a profligate to that of a saint. In Spenser and Milton the break with the life of the senses is never complete, and so we feel a tension in their works between personality traits which are either puritanical or oversexed. In our own period, Thomas Mann's artist figures veer between frustrated sex and great art, and the protagonists are both puritanical and licentious, by fits.[14] In Shaw, we see a gradual movement from a most passionate involvement with music (and cycling) to a Platonism whose goal, after exhausting the pleasure to be derived from contemplation of the properties of numbers, is a rigid stasis in the universe of Ideas. Plato banishes poetry from his Republic because he is afraid of lowering the floodgates that admit more birth, copulation, and death than absolutely necessary. Shaw's utopianism is from the same school. His fear of the purely arty is the fear of what the flutes might do to the soldiers in the Republic. For Shaw, those works of art are acceptable which seem to lead to the stasis of his utopia, while those works which merely titillate the senses are unacceptable because they lure us back to the lower rungs of the Platonic ladder, the rungs of desires that can never be satisfied because they are always starting all over again, like wild and self-destructive bicycle rides.

The two major views, then, which Shaw's critics take of his personality and his art have a good deal of validity. Their limitation is that they assume there is no more to Shaw's character and sensibility than the description they have offered of one of the warring elements of the whole. Shaw *is* an ascetic, a Platonist, and possibly a mystic in a loose sense; but he *is also* a voluptuary, a sensualist (albeit a refined one), an esthete. The conflict results in an estheticism which eschews pleasure divorced from a prospect of the ultimate stasis toward which mankind itself partially strives (e.g., Christian immortality), and a Platonism which scorns the sort of mere rationalism that denies or ignores the role of the emotions and the will in human activity. Indeed, Shaw's doctrine of the will, adopted and transmuted from Schopenhauer, is an explicit acknowledgment on his part of the predominance of emotion and irrationality as motives for human actions, a predominance which he is not prepared to give up.

In practice, this dualism appears in Shaw's writings and in his daily activities as a program for cultivating as many of the faculties as possible, so that art, ideas, and practical life may be perfected to approximate the ideal world, the world which he is preoccupied with so explicitly in *Back to Methuselah*.[15]

The Aims of the Drama

Shaw did not believe in having a "good time." The only genuinely recreative activities for a man who lives in high gear are those activities which exhilarate his higher faculties. For Shaw, it is unthinkable to have "fun" for its own sake. For "fun" is actually boring and depressing when you can listen to Wagner instead. Shaw continually complained that the theater of his day did not offer high-level experiences to the playgoer who sought them. "People dont go to the theatre to be pleased. . . . One likes something solid." And what is solid? "Salutary self-torture" (III, 246)! If someone should object that people do not go to the theater to learn or to suffer torture, Shaw would reply that "play-going is at bottom as utilitarian as washing" (II, 72). When Shaw uses the word "utilitarian" he does not mean "unesthetic," although Chesterton supposes as much. The esthetic experience is, far from being non-utilitarian, indispensable to a sane life.[16] If one considers the church, there is no contradiction between utilitarian and esthetic. That is how Shaw looked at the drama. When he published his collected drama reviews in 1906, he prefaced them with the remark: "A theatre to me is a place 'where two or three are gathered together.' The apostolic succession from Eschylus to myself is as serious and as continuously inspired as that younger institution, the apostolic succession of the Christian Church" (I, vi). When he goes on to speak of the theater as "a temple of the Ascent of Man" (I, vii), the flavor of nineteenth-century philosophy is distinct. One of Shaw's critics points out that Shaw's dislike of the English Renaissance drama "is chiefly a criticism of the Renaissance tragedy of the individual, a tragic view without the religious or social basis of Greek tragedy or the moralistic purpose of medieval drama."[17] In an amusing letter to William T. Stead in 1894—a man who never went to the theater—Shaw wrote: "What a man you are—to talk of making a round of the theatres, as if they were brothels! . . .

However, if you begin, you had better begin with the most serious attempt yet made to treat the theatre as a temple—I mean, of course, Bayreuth."[18]

Shaw is explicit about the moral purpose of the theater when he says that the aim of his plays is to woo a man's soul instead of having some sweet heroine woo a handsome young man in order to marry him.[19] (It is interesting that one of the central problems of Shaw's own plays is the conflict between salvation and sex; in Shaw salvation never comes through romantic love, as it does in D. H. Lawrence.) "The schoolboy who, having seen my play, told his headmaster that he could pray to St Joan but not to Jesus Christ, justified the theatre as one of the most vital of public institutions."[20] And in a letter, Shaw wrote: "I want to write a big book of devotion for modern people, bringing all the truths latent in the old religious dogmas into contact with real life—a gospel of Shawianity, in fact."[21]

If the theater is the modern church, it must not give the people what they want but what is good for them.

Even if the public really knew what it likes and what it dislikes—a consummation of wisdom which it is as far from as any child—the true master-dramatist would still give it, not what it likes, but what is good for it. (I, 267-68)

The drama's laws the drama's patrons do not give, nor ever can give: that is the prerogative of the dramatist, and of the dramatist alone. Nor need anybody "please to live": on the contrary, the person who is willing to do anything to please everyone is a universally and deservedly despised and disastrous person. The public cannot do without the theatre; and the actor and the dramatist are therefore in a position to insist on honorable terms. (I, 228)

The antithesis between the church and the stage was one which Shaw could not abide. He constantly raged against those puritans who regarded art as a department of Original Sin, and he claimed instead that art in all its forms was a department of religion.[22] "The work of insisting that the church is the house of God and the theatre the house of Satan may be left to those poor North Sea islanders who have been brought up to believe that it is wrong to enter a playhouse. The theatre is really the week-day church; and a good play is essentially identical with a church service as a combination of artistic ritual, profession of faith, and sermon" (I, 263-64). Although Christianity has lost its vitality, religion is not dead, said Shaw, for modern European literature and music provide a new Bible "far surpassing in importance to us the Ancient Hebrew Bible that has served us so long." Inspiration and revelation, far from being exhausted in some dim past, are vouchsafed to creative genius as much now as ever (*Essays*, p. 147). "I am myself a literary artist, and have made larger claims for literature—or, at any rate, put them forward more explicitly—than any writer of my generation as far as I know, claiming a continuous inspiration for modern literature of precisely the same character as that conceded to the ancient Hebrew Scriptures, and maintaining that the man of letters, when he is more than a mere confectioner, is a prophet or nothing" (*Pen Portraits*, p. 232).[23]

Since the major modern problem is not man's relation to God but man's relation to society, the modern drama is most in tune with contemporary civilization when it deals with social questions. As Shaw saw it, a social problem of the greatest interest and importance was the emancipation of the individual from the blind tyranny of popular conventions. In Shaw's own plays, this takes the form of a superior and gifted individualist who flouts the conventions of his class. And insofar as Shaw was able to detect this theme in Ibsen's plays, he became an admirer of Ibsen. Social problems are filtered into the drama because "If people are rotting and starving in all directions, and nobody else has the heart or brains to make a disturbance about it, the great writers must."[24] But Shaw candidly admits that most social dramas lose their interest after the problems they deal with are eliminated. He even goes so far as to say that "A Doll's House will be as flat as ditchwater when A Midsummer Night's Dream will still be as fresh as paint; but it will have done more work in the world; and that is enough for the highest genius, which is always intensely utilitarian."[25] Yet this mania for usefulness is the mania to make life into art. For Shaw, as I have attempted to show, art was not a substitute for life—it was a model according to which the world was to transform itself. William Irvine writes: "The only art in which Shaw seems inclined to value an abstract and useless beauty is music, and even there he admires most a composer like Wagner who brings his work into closer and more practical relation to life. [A somewhat dark statement.] Beauty is holy when joined with utility. Transient beauty with utility surpasses lasting beauty without."[26]

The Old Drama and the New

The pre-Ibsen drama, against which Shaw rebelled, appeared to him a distorted mirror of nature, suitable for childish fantasies, but falling far short of penetrating psychology. In Garrick's day, the charm of the theater consisted in its make-believe. But make-believe is undesirable (*Prefaces*, p. 112). The popular dramatists achieved their successes through a simple formula: they would "pour another kettle-full of water on the exhausted tea-leaves of romance" (III, 346) or appeal to stock patriotic-heroic emotions in the audience, or, much worse, play the game of idealized sex. In an uproarious review of a romance by Rostand, Shaw wrote:

A first act in which the men do nothing but describe their hysterical visions of a wonderful goddess-princess whom they have never seen is bad enough; but it is pardonable, because men do make fools of themselves about women, sometimes in an interesting and poetic fashion. But when the woman appears and plays up to the height of their folly, intoning her speeches to an accompaniment of harps and horns, distributing lilies and languors to pilgrims, and roses and raptures to troubadours, always in the character which their ravings have ascribed to her, what can one feel except that an excellent opportunity for a good comedy is being thrown away? If Melisinde would only eat something, or speak prose, or only swear in it, or do anything human—were it even smoking a cigaret—to bring these silly Argonauts to their senses for a moment, one could forgive her. But she remains an unredeemed humbug from one end of the play to the other. (I, 154-55)

Shaw makes fun of most of the romantic and chivalric conventions of popular drama—and in the light of his reviews of military plays, one sees where the inspiration arose for *Arms and the Man*. Wherever a noble but absurd sentiment would appear in a conventional heroic play, Shaw put a commonsensical sentiment in his own play.

"Don't talk to me of romances: I was sent into the world expressly to dance on them with thick boots."[27]

Indeed, Shaw was always quarreling with William Archer about Archer's sentimentality. After they had agreed to collaborate in writing a play to be called "Rheingold," Shaw took the matter in hand and ended up with *Widowers' Houses*, having ditched Archer altogether along the way. In a letter explaining what he had done to *their* play, Shaw told Archer, "You will perceive that my genius has brought the romantic notion which possessed you, into vivid contact with real life."[28] Archer always misunderstood Shaw's own writings as a habit of dwelling on "the seamy side" of human nature, which Shaw defended as "realism."[29]

The entire set of stage conventions seemed to Shaw to be evasions of reality for people who could not bear to look upon real life. Eventually, the artificialities of the stage begin to appear "natural" to habitual theatergoers. But repetition of anything dulls the critical faculty, and to a person who is made to stand on his head for twenty-four hours a day, head-standing must come to seem natural. "When any art drifts into that phase of extreme artificiality in which its touch with contemporary life is lost, the ensuing reaction to natural subjects and straightforward lifelike methods—the Return to Nature, as we say—may be welcome enough to the world at large; but it invariably and inevitably produces on the case-hardened professional critic an impression of perverse and outrageous violation of custom, undertaken wantonly in a spirit of mischief or as a bid for notoriety."[30] Even critics lose their judgment once they get settled in their seats and assume that it is " 'natural' for clergymen to be saintly, for soldiers to be heroic" (*Prefaces*, p. 232). The customary conflicts of popular drama are between animal passion and a set of conventions "half of which do not exist off the stage, whilst the other half can either be evaded . . . or defied with complete impunity by any reasonably strong-minded person" (*Prefaces*, p. 228). Even tragedy is unrealistic, for it comes down to us from the days "when life was so thoroughly accepted as a divine institution that in order to make it seem tragic, something dreadful had to happen and somebody had to die. But the tragedy of modern life is that nothing happens, and that the resultant dulness does not kill" (*Prefaces*, p. 199). Nowadays, no serious dramatist could undertake to write a conventional tragedy, because "modern commercialism is a bad art school, and cannot, with all its robberies, murders and prostitutions, move us in the grand manner to pity and terror" (*Prefaces*, p. 703).

The great curse and cause of popular romance and tragedy is too little contact with real life and too much contact with books. If a writer hopes to produce a drama of substance, he has to stop reading other romantic plays and begin to look on real life with a fresh eye (III, 170-71, 181-82). One of the faults which Shaw found with university education (he was always on the defensive about higher education,[31] since he had none himself) was that too much contact with books and too little experience of daily realities produces erudite ignoramuses. Of a pair of plays he had just seen he wrote: "They have the defect of being second-hand: that is to say, they have the unreality, and consequently the tediousness, of the images which the imagination produces when, instead of being solidly fed on experience, it is merely excited by the contemplation of other works of art" (II, 98).

The aim of great drama is not to sweeten a few idle hours with pretty illusions but to make some sense of the chaos of daily life. What the dramatist must do is to give up accidents, catastrophies, and romantic lies, and take slices of life as his subject matter. Doing this will result in plays that have no situation and no ending. Romance must be swept away—it is "a product of *ennui*, an attempt to escape from a condition in which real life appears empty, prosaic, and boresome" (III, 170), and it panders to "that miserable vital incapacity to which life at its imagined best means only what a confectioner's shop window means to a child" (III, 227). It is what he calls a "classical" drama that Shaw was seeking. "What I mean by classical is that he [the dramatist] can present a dramatic hero as a man whose passions are those which have produced the philosophy, the poetry, the art, and the statecraft of the world, and not merely those which have produced its weddings, coroners' inquests, and executions" (III, 201). The true comedy and tragedy of modern life is the conflict between romantic ideals and hard reality, which refuses to conform to those ideals. The most advanced audiences of the nineties (as opposed to the popular audiences), taught as they were by Wagner, Ibsen, and Goethe, "cannot stand the drop back into decoration after the moment of earnest life. They want realistic drama of complete brainy, passional texture all through" (III, 194).

What is real, what is earnest, what is passionate for Shaw is the evolution of the Life Force—that is, man's latest intellectual advance in his great ascent. While the sluggish masses are still living according to the old, outworn thesis, the dramatist must be incarnating into art the latest antithesis. Though well-presented fantasy will always have an audience, "the best plays are those made of the very stuff of contemporary life in its most deeply felt aspects."[32] Shaw summed this up vigorously in one of his letters:

Caesar and Cleopatra is an attempt of mine to pay an installment of the debt that all dramatists owe to the art of heroic acting. Since Shakespeare paid up so handsomely on this score, the British drama has been falling into heavier and heavier arrears. . . . Besides, our conception of heroism has changed of late years. The stage hero of the palmy days is a pricked bubble. The gentlemanly hero, of whom Tennyson's King Arthur was the type, suddenly found himself out, as Torvald Helmer in Ibsen's *Doll's House*, and died of the shock. It is no use now going on with heroes who are no longer really heroic to us. Besides, we want credible heroes. The old demand for the incredible, the impossible, the superhuman, which was supplied by bombast, inflation and the piling of crimes on catastrophes and factitious raptures on artificial agonies, has fallen off; and the demand now is for heroes in whom we can recognize our own humanity, and who, instead of walking, talking, eating, drinking, sleeping, making love and fighting single combats in a monotonous ecstasy of continuous heroism, are heroic in the true human fashion: that is, touching the summits only at rare moments, and finding the proper level of all occasions, condescending with humour and good sense to the prosaic ones, as well as rising to the noble ones, instead of ridiculously persisting in rising to them all on the principle that a hero must always soar, in season and out of season.[33]

Even more characteristic of the old romantic drama than twenty-four-hour heroes were twenty-four-hour villains. One has only to look at Iago, said Shaw, for a specimen of villainy scarcely resembling human nature at all. The tradition of the stage for hundreds of years has been a tradition of such full-time good men and bad men. But in real life no man says, "Evil: be thou my good" (II, 3-4). Plenty of impressive villainy can be obtained through a representation of the lives of ordinary ladies and gentlemen—one does not have to create monsters, since part of us all is monstrous. Shaw regarded the stage villain as a "*diabolus ex machina*" (*Prefaces*, p. 631), and since Shakespeare is full of villains, Shaw was not fond of Shakespeare's tragedies, for they did not seem to be representations of real life. The secret of a true-to-life drama is that it recognizes the mixture of good and evil in human nature.[34] "Nature does not keep heroism exclusively for one set of men and villainy exclusively for another, merely to enable us all to become dramatists and 'paint character' with a bucket of whitewash and a jar of lampblack" (*Prefaces*, p. 705).

Instead of villains and heroes, if our dramas are to be realistic, says Shaw, we must exploit Schopenhauer's discovery of the Will: the irrational impulse is everything, the rational faculties nothing. "The intellect by itself is a dead piece of brain machinery, and our ethical and moral systems merely the pierced cards you stick into it to make it play a certain tune" (II, 94). Idiosyncrasy, will, passion, impulse—not reason—are the mainsprings of action. "The will that moves us is dogmatic . . . our brain is only the very imperfect instrument by which we devise practical means for fulfilling that will . . . the man who gives to reason and logic the attributes and authority of the will—the Rationalist— is the most hopeless of fools" (*Pen Portraits*, p. 88).

The underlying psychology of Shaw's thought and dramas is Schopenhauer's doctrine, from *The World as Will and Idea*, that desire is the motive force of human life and that reason merely justifies and helps to satisfy one's will. "The ordinary man, leading the ordinary life," Shaw writes in 1889, "never becomes conscious of the will or impulse in him that sets his brain to work at devising ways and reasons. He supposes his life to be a mere matter of logical consequences from a few bodily appetites and externally appointed 'duties' with their attendant pains and penalties."[35] Ultimately, then, an irrational compulsion determines behavior. "The irresistibility of a chain of logic lies, not in the logic, but in the acceptability of the conclusion to the person addressed."[36] However, there is a radical distinction to be made between Schopenhauer's doctrine of will and Shaw's. Schopenhauer was a complete pessimist, for whom will was a curse, an Ixion's wheel of endless torment due to insatiable desires. Suicide was the only direct remedy, but asceticism—as well as drowning oneself in music—were secondary means of relief. (This casts light, by the by, on Shaw's personality.) But Shaw regarded will as a good thing, as the motive power of the Life Force. Whereas life was revolting to Schopenhauer, to Shaw it was worthy of celebration. (Suspiciously, however, Shaw ends up as a Platonist, a very life-denying position.) In a letter to William Archer, Shaw explained how his own views differed from those of Schopenhauer: "I have taken his distinction between the intellect and the will. . . . That does not make me a Schopenhaurist, or Ibsen one. His pessimism, and his conviction that the will was the devil and the intellect the divine saviour, marks him off from me and from Ibsen in the clearest and most fundamental way. You might just as well call me a Herbert Spencerist because I accept the doctrine of evolution."[37] Eric Bentley summarizes Shaw's position well: "Like Nietzsche, Shaw saw that one could digest

Schopenhauer's 'irrationalism' and put the pessimism back on the plate. To Nietzsche and Shaw the essence of Schopenhauer was his contention that the Will is the main driving-force of human existence. To equate this Will with the Christian Soul, as Shaw does, is certainly an act of faith, but so is equating it with the Freudian Id as Thomas Mann does. Schopenhauer found the Will horrifying; Shaw finds it inspiring."[38]

Women's irrationality does not prevent their arriving at the right conclusions, Shaw notes, and when they begin to ratiocinate too freely, they merely fall into the errors which men usually fall into (*Essays*, p. 19). After all, he goes on to observe, if we were really rational we would all commit suicide, especially when life becomes more unbearable than usual—but the Will to Live keeps us among the living, even though reason can see the only wise course. The Will is primary, given, absolute. Everything can be explained in terms of it, but it cannot be explained in terms of anything, since everything presupposes it. Therefore, a realistic drama must show us "the naïve feeling underlying the ideas" (II, 192), for the ideas themselves are embroidery, not substance. When the critics were baffled by Dick Dudgeon's attempt to sacrifice himself for the Reverend Mr. Anderson, they asked: Why did he do it? Shaw replied: "On the stage, it appears, people do things for reasons. Off the stage they dont" (*Prefaces*, p. 747). "The unconscious self is the real genius" (*Prefaces*, p. 193).

Although a realistic drama must be built upon realistic psychology, the dramatist is permitted the license granted to other artists, namely, to make his art more intelligible than daily life. Thus, the characters, even in a realistic play, are of necessity more self-aware than people in ordinary life, "for by no other means can they be made intelligible to the audience" (*Prefaces*, p. 631). "It is the privilege of the drama to make life intelligible, at least hypothetically, by introducing moral design into it, even if that design be only to shew that moral design is an illusion" (III, 18-19). In *Man and Superman*, for example, we have John Tanner both a spokesman for and victim of the Life Force. Of course, since Shavian drama enjoys sermonizing, the characters are unusually self-aware.[39]

Life Force: Agents and Methods

With the crude psychology of heroes and villains proscribed, and with the new psychology of the unconscious will prescribed, the job of civilization is to detect unconscious impulses and destroy the obsolete codifications that no longer fit the realities. This, if anything, is the main activity of Shavian drama—the so-called ripping off the veils in order to expose the substance underneath. *Sartor Resartus* would serve as an excellent primer to Shavian philosophy once Schopenhauer had been digested. But this continual revelation of self is not mere change—it is development, it is civilization. The later self is more aware than any of the earlier selves, whether the later self is a man of fifty looking back at his youth or the twentieth century looking back at the fifteenth. Both can think more thoughts because the repertoire of thoughts keeps increasing. "The creative Energy, as yet neither omnipotent nor omniscient, but ever striving to become both, proceeds by the method of trial and error, and has still something to live for" (*Pen Portraits*, p. 158). Shaw liked Ibsen's *Emperor and Galilean* because it told him that "the Kingdom of heaven is within YOU": For

48

Shaw, Ibsen was saying that *man* is God. Although he is not yet omniscient or omnipotent, he is constantly arriving closer to being so, for knowledge truly is power. (The heroes of Shaw's plays usually know more than the other characters and are consequently unruffled.)

We can see why Shaw became involved in social problems and in sociological drama: outworn convention and hollow taboos are hindrances to knowledge and are therefore evil. The moral obligation of the agent of the Life Force is to overthrow these old bonds so that the latest stage in man's development may express itself and be known. In the nineteenth century this produced a "movement" which Shaw called Diabolism. All of the devils were his angels: Ibsen, Nietzsche, Wagner, and, naturally, Shaw (*Pen Portraits*, pp. 217-20). But since these moralists lacked respectability (which consists in lauding the established order) they were regarded as immoral, immorality, by Shaw's definition, being merely the insistence on ideas which are contrary to those established in society. Shaw relished such utterances as "I am not an ordinary playwright. . . . I am a specialist in immoral and heretical plays. My reputation has been gained by my persistent struggle to force the public to reconsider its morals" (*Prefaces*, p. 410). Eric Bentley, using Shaw's own words, has described his plays as depictions of the "struggle between human vitality and the artificial system of morality."[40] Shaw's vaunted immorality, and the heretical doctrines of his plays, are epitomized in statements like this: "The fact is, armies as we know them are made possible, not by valor in the rank and file, but by the lack of it; not by physical courage . . . but by civic impotence and moral cowardice. I am afraid of a soldier, not because he is a brave man, but

49

because he is so utterly unmanned by discipline that he will kill me if he is told. . . . I respect a regiment for a mutiny more than for a hundred victories."[41] Rebellion, far from being vicious, is the only virtue: "Integrity consists in obeying the morality which you accept" (I, 176). The conscientious objector, then, is the hero, not the soldier who fights in the field because he is afraid of what society will do to him if he refuses. When Golding Bright, following Shaw's advice, told his father to cut off his allowance, Shaw wrote: "I congratulate you especially on the fact that all your friends and relations regard you as a madman. That is an indispensable beginning to a respectable, independent life."[42] "Though we may not all care to say so, yet it is the rebel against society who interests us; and we want to see the rebel triumphant rather than crushed or reconciled" (I, 234). The rebel is most likely to be an agent of the Life Force, because he is most likely to fight for the latest expression of man's soul against the outworn but accepted expression of a prior soul. A good portion of *The Sanity of Art* deals with the problem of the genius who is exempt from conventional morality and legality and who, instead, makes his own. Most people are content to follow the established customs, not only for the sake of a quiet life, as Shaw would say, but for the simple reason that they know no better. Laws "are made necessary, though we all secretly detest them, by the fact that the number of people who can think out a line of conduct for themselves even on one point is very small" (*Essays*, pp. 304-05). Even a genius accepts more conventions than he is aware of, merely for the sake of convenience. But on essential issues, in matters of conscience, the genius will rebel rather than follow the code. And in this way the Life Force triumphs over the repressive forces of convention: "Law soon acquires such a good character that people will believe no evil of it; and at this point it becomes possible for priests and rulers to commit the most pernicious crimes in the name of law and order. Creeds and laws come to be regarded as applications to human conduct of eternal and immutable principles of good and evil; and breakers of the law are abhorred as sacrilegious scoundrels to whom nothing is sacred" (*Essays*, p. 307). Creative evolution, however, moves from submission and obedience, to willfulness and rebellious self-assertion (*Essays*, p. 308).

Sylvan Barnet, explaining the relation of this evolution to the role of comedy, observes that traditional comedy censures deviations from convention, while Shaw believed that "allegiance to a code is necessarily ludicrous, for it becomes outdated. His comic hero, then, develops, or adopts, a new realistic morality beyond that of his society's idealism. Shavian comedy is critical not of individuals but of society's norm, insisting that the individual who pierces illusions is not absurd but in line with the process of the world spirit."[43] The root of much of Shaw's criticism of the so-called problem plays of his own day, especially those of Pinero, is to be found in this view of evolution and its relation to comedy. Much of the material on which supposedly serious dramatists based their "problems" would actually have been fit for satiric treatment in comedy.

An interesting sidelight on comedy is Shaw's perception of the shift in comic materials during the past several hundred years. As the Life Force refines the mind, subjects that were once treated as hilarious jokes come to be treated as questions of serious morality.

Shaw himself uses *The School for Scandal* to point this out: Sheridan's play is dated because "Joseph's virtue is a pretence instead of a reality, and because the women in the play are set apart and regarded as absolutely outside the region of free judgment in which the men act."

What now jars on us is the caddishness of Lady Teazle, whose conduct for the first time begins to strike us as it would if it were the conduct of a man in the like circumstances. Society forbids a man to compromise a woman; but it also requires him, if he nevertheless does compromise her, to accept as one of the consequences of his action the obligation not to betray her, even if he has to go into the witness-box and swear to her innocence. Suppose Lady Teazle, on being surprised by Sir Peter in Joseph's rooms, had invented a plausible excuse, and had asked Joseph to confirm her. Suppose Joseph had thereupon said, "No, it is false, every word. My slumbering conscience awakens; and I return to the sacred path of truth and duty. Your wife, Sir Peter, is an abandoned woman who came here to tempt me from the path of honor. . . ." Would any extremity of blackballing, cutting, even kicking, be considered too severe for the man who should try to extricate himself at the expense of his accomplice in that straightforward manner? And yet that is exactly what Lady Teazle does without the least misgivings on the part of the dramatist as to the entire approval and sympathy of the audience. In this, as far as I am concerned, the dramatist is mistaken, and the play consequently dates. I cannot for the life of me see why it is less dishonorable for a woman to kiss and tell than a man. (II, 168-69)

A modern comedy, written with the benefit of more years of the Life Force at work, would treat the same scene ironically, exposing the hypocrisy of the double standard. For "the function of comedy is to dispel . . . unconsciousness by turning the searchlight of the keenest moral and intellectual analysis right on to it" (III, 84). If comedy, then, "is nothing less than the destruction of old-established morals" (III, 87), it is surely another agent of the Life Force.

As we see in Shaw's treatment of Shakespeare, not only pure comedy, but tragicomedy too, is able to deal with the points of view which interest Shaw. He believed that comedy, and especially tragicomedy, had replaced tragedy as the main force of the drama, chastening behavior through irony, though not through ridicule.[44] Shaw's use of comedy is explained well by Daniel Bernd: "Shaw is comic, humorous, and ironic, but not satirical. Shaw is not satirical . . . for the very simple reason that he did not think it the function of comedy, or any other form of the drama, to administer pain. This is not so surprising when we consider Shaw's ethical position on a broad range of subjects. He objected to punishment, revenge, vivisection, blood sports, killing of animals for food, capital punishment, and any form of cruelty whatever, and more often than not, his objections were based on the evil effects on the perpetrator as much as on the victim."[45]

If geniuses and comedies are chief agents of the Life Force, what are the means whereby an individual can cultivate the Life Force within himself? With will and impulse—not reason—as the mainspring of human life, it is necessary to refine one's emotional and sensuous susceptibilities if one wishes to live at the highest possible level of one's being. This imperative is perfectly in character, coming, as it does, from an esthete, "voluptuary," and puritan:

Taking it, then, as established that life is a curse to us unless it operates as pleasurable activity, and that as it becomes more intense with the upward evolution of the race it requires a degree of pleasure which cannot be extracted from the alimentary, predatory, and amatory instincts without ruinous perversions of them; seeing, also, that the alternative of "high thinking" is impossible until it is started by "high feeling," to which we can only come through the education of the senses —are we to deliberately reverse our own Puritan traditions and aim at becoming a nation of skilled voluptuaries? Certainly.[46]

Shaw tells us in his *Sixteen Self Sketches* that he valued sexual experience mainly because its ecstasy was a foretaste of what normal life would be like after the Life Force had been at work for a very long time. Elsewhere he said that in some dim future men will "experience a sustained ecstasy of thought that will make our sexual ecstasies seem child's play,"[47] a subject dealt with in *Back to Methuselah*. Of paramount importance, however, is the fact that feeling precedes thought and that one's feelings must be cultivated before one can have a refined mind. Shaw unconsciously paraphrases another voluptuary-puritan, John Milton (who said that Spenser was a better teacher than Aquinas), when he asks: "Which is the greater education, pray—your tutor, when he coaches you for the Ireland scholarship or Miss Janet Achurch, when she plays Nora for you?"[48] The aim of this refinement of the senses is a phenomenon even higher than thought: mystic ecstasy. Nowhere is this made clearer than in an inspiring flight from "The Religion of the Pianoforte":

However you may despise romantic novels, however loftily you may be absorbed in the future destiny of what is highest in humanity, so that for mere light literature you turn from Dante to Goethe, or from Schopenhauer to Comte, or from Ruskin to Ibsen— still, if you do not know *Die Zauberflöte*, if you have never soared into the heaven where they sing the choral ending of the Ninth Symphony, if *Der Ring des Nibelungen* is nothing to you but a newspaper phrase, then you are an ignoramus, however eagerly you may pore in your darkened library over the mere printed labels of those wonders that can only be communicated by the transubstantiation of pure feeling for musical tone [*sic*].[49]

Schopenhauer would not have dissented.

Art and Sex

The Life Force, as we gather from a reading of *Man and Superman*, works through sex to achieve its ends, but its ends are intellect joined with sensibility—we might call it "soul." Now, as Schopenhauer has brilliantly pointed out, sex is the first, last, and intermediate infirmity of the Will to Live, as it appears in most people. But, like all other appetites, it is a great destroyer of intellect and judgment. That is, things which our minds in cool moments would scorn are avidly relished in moments of gratification. Food and mates are equally unappetizing after satiety. But Wagner is always appetizing. As long as we are forced to enjoy the gratification of appetites which our keener wit must regard as ridiculous, we must enjoy them, said Shaw, quite apart from the realm of moral and intellectual judgments, which do not apply to matters of private feelings. For Shaw, passion, that is, subjection to the Will to Live at a low level, could not possibly inspire great or significant emotions or art, because it is the result of a transient physiological condition. That is

55

why Dick Dudgeon's offer to sacrifice himself is such a striking artistic achievement: it was not appetite for Judith which caused it, but outrageous integrity. For Shaw, *intellect* was a passion: "The search for enlightenment of any sort is far more interesting and enduring than, say, the sexual pursuit of a woman by a man."[50] But Shaw discerned that most people disliked art except as an aphrodisiac. "Fine Art throughout the world is only known to a few people as being a really good thing, as being an edifying thing, as being a necessary part of civilization."[51] He believed that the ecstasy of *Tristan*, for example, entirely surpassed sex because the experience of *Tristan* is the uttermost fruit of consciousness, rather than unconsciousness. The aims of art, he has said, are to cultivate, refine, and extend the ranges of our senses and faculties, and this is essentially a spiritual extension—it is, in a word, the goal of the Life Force. This is why Shaw was usually so grim about sex—sex to him was an evil necessary to refine the race—preferably through eugenics, but at least through the trial and error of the Life Force—into a population capable of regarding the orgy of *Tristan* as superior to real orgies. To be sidetracked along the wayside by trifling delights is to return to pre-Neanderthal days. As Joad points out, Shaw thought art should supersede, not glorify, sex.[52] And as Shaw himself remembered: "I have a technical objection to making sexual infatuation a tragic theme. Experience proves that it is only effective in the comic spirit" (*Prefaces*, p. 749).

Theater managers, however, are interested primarily in money, and so, heedless of the Life Force, they fall back "on the instinct of sex as the avenue to all hearts" (*Prefaces*, p. 739). That is why Ibsen was not popular among them: "Can I be expected to refrain from laughing at the spectacle of a number of respectable gentlemen lamenting because a playwright lures them to the theatre by a promise to excite their senses . . . and then, having successfully trapped them . . . proceeds to ignore their senses and ruthlessly improve their minds?" (*Prefaces*, p. 227). Particularly offensive to Shaw was farcical sexual comedy, with its stale jokes about "tarts" (II, 217) and its opportunities for interpolation of indecencies by the actors to make their roles a success (II, 164).

One of the strongest objections to the institution of monogamy is the existence of its offspring, the conventional farcical comedy. The old warning, "Beware how you kiss when you do not love," ought to be paraphrased on the playbills of all our lighter theatres as "Beware how you laugh when you do not enjoy." To laugh without sympathy is a ruinous abuse of a noble function; and the degradation of any race may be measured by the degree of their addiction to it. . . . To produce high art in the theatre, the author must create persons whose fortunes we can follow as those of a friend or enemy: to produce base laughter, it is only necessary to turn human beings on to the stage as rats are turned into a pit, that they may be worried for the entertainment of the spectators. (II, 118-19)

And after a performance consisting of much female display, he quipped: "Two minutes of Biarritz would reconcile a Trappist to his monastery for life" (II, 104).

The sexual farce that Shaw condemned most frequently was a production entitled *Gentleman Joe*, which he attended in 1895. He never quite recovered from seeing this performance, for he alluded to it for

57

practically the rest of his life. Immediately after seeing it, he wrote:

It is impossible to sit out an entertainment like Gentleman Joe without reflecting on the enormous part played in the theatre by hypnotic suggestion. At what point I fall a victim to it myself I, of course, do not know. No "professor" in the world can persuade me that a glass of paraffin oil is a bumper of Imperial Tokay. But as I look back on my earliest impressions of certain performances which completely dominated my imagination, I have to admit that my view of them was very far from being a sane and objective one. And now that it is my business as a critic to gain such a sane and objective view over the whole field of art, I sometimes find myself at the theatre in a state of distressingly complete sanity among neighbors who are in the wildest ecstasies at nothing. This was my predicament at Gentleman Joe. . . . [Regarding the comedian Arthur Roberts:] And again, when, wishing to convey to the audience that one of the persons on the stage was beside himself, he tapped his forehead and said, "Balmy on the crumpet," I, having long ago exhausted such delight as lurks in that fantastic expression, heaved a sigh amid the general laughter. I do not deny that these sallies are funny in comparison with absolute vacuity; but surely, since private life supplies rather more than enough of them free of charge, one need not go to the trouble and expense of a visit to the theatre to procure them. Then there were certain humors which probably made a majority of the audience uneasy, and were not witty enough to excuse the company for condescending to them. For example, Mr Roberts, as Gentleman Joe, the hansom cabby, comes to see his sweetheart. He says to the butler, "Where's Emma?" The butler replies, "Emma is getting ready to see you, and is taking off her things." Mr Roberts receives this in such a way as to shew that the line may be construed to mean that the young lady is undressing herself completely; and the house, pleased at its own cleverness in finding this out, and at Mr Roberts' artfulness in suggesting it, laughs at the schoolboy indecency for fully half a minute. Again, Mr Roberts is conversing with Miss Kitty Loftus, the sweetheart aforesaid, who has a piece of frilling in her hand. He asks her what it is. "That," she tells him, "is frilling for me to wear." "Where?" he asks; and as "where" and "wear" make a sort of pun, there is a faint laugh from the quicker wits present. "In my hat," is Miss Loftus's answer. Whereupon Mr Roberts, by appropriate pantomine, makes it appear that he had supposed the frilling to belong to her undergarments; and there is again a huge guffaw. Now this sort of thing is to me mere silly misbehavior, and I want to have it banished from the stage. (I, 55-56)

Shaw then asks how it can be banished—the actor has supplied the first joke, so the Censor cannot read it, and the second joke is ignored by the Censor. The only solution is the taste of the comedian. Elsewhere he has written: "We have dramatists who write their lines in such a way as to enable low comedians of a certain class to give them an indecorous turn" (Essays, p. 316), evidently with the present instance in mind. And what makes the objection even stronger, is that all the while the dirty business is going on, supplied mostly by the actor, the play complies in a shallow way with conventional notions of morality.

At the same time, I am of opinion that these entertainments would be far more enjoyable if they were not so depressingly moral. Let them be courageously written from the point of view of the devil's advocate; and

59

then there will be conviction in them, interest in them, and wit in them. For example, I have not the slightest objection to Yvette Guilbert singing Les Vierges. In that song you hear virtue attacked with bitter irony by a poet who does not believe in it and—I must not say by an artist who does not believe in it either, but at all events by one who has the power of throwing herself with mordant intensity into the poet's attitude for the moment. Let us by all means have whole plays written like Les Vierges, in which the votaries of pleasure can religiously put forward their creed against idealists and the Puritans. There would be life in that—purpose, honesty, reality, and the decency which arises spontaneously beside them. But a timidly conventional play like Gentleman Joe, with its abject little naughtinesses furtively slipped in under cover of the tamest propriety, and with a pitiful whoop at the end about a debauched clergyman riding in a cab with a lady, of whom Mr Roberts sings

> Perhaps she was his aunt,
> Or another Mrs Chant,

—all this is about as lively as the performances of the children who make faces at their teachers in Sunday-school. (I, 58-59)

Shaw once again had this play in mind, when he wrote in one of his prefaces: "With all their labored efforts to keep up an understanding of furtive naughtiness between the low comedian on the stage and the drunken undergraduate in the stalls, they insisted all the time on their virtue and patriotism and loyalty" (Prefaces, pp. 739-40).

William Archer's review of Gentleman Joe in The Theatrical 'World' of 1895 reveals a similar reaction to the play: "They faced each other in pairs, and set to jigging it—grown men and women—not in figures, not in elaborate steps, not pretending to express any emotion or any dramatic idea, but simply bobbing up and down to the music." Of the joke about the woman taking her things off, Archer wrote: "But Mr. Arthur Roberts, by the artful intonation of his 'Oh!' helped out with a leer and a grimace, converts the innocent remark into an indecency as palpable as it is senseless. The censor who cannot keep the low comedian in order is of very little avail."[53]

The other type of sex offense on the stage which Shaw often complained about was the fake sexuality of woman-with-a-past plays. There is very little frank treatment of sex on the stage, Shaw used to say. There is plenty of legal entanglement resulting from sex, divorce cases, court scenes, and social horror at women with pasts, but nothing is ever written about genuinely sexual matters per se. The preface to Mrs. Warren's Profession deals with this at length, and Man and Superman, as Shaw tells us in that preface, is the first modern sex play in English. Although even Shaw's "realistic" plays are somewhat far from any familiar reality, they do often discuss sex in a frank and unabashed manner which was new to the theater of his day. The general complaint is that Shaw's sex plays are sexless, but it would be more accurate to say that his plays avoid romantic sex and aphrodisiac stimulation, for, as a matter of fact, they deal with sex all the time. The seriousness of treatment and the lack of romantic and conventional attitudes toward sex are sufficient to make the plays seem sexless to audiences who want vicarious sexual experience from art forms such as drama. In the final analysis, Shaw's view of sex, both in his criticism and in his plays, is dignified and serious in the way that the Greek and Roman view is dignified and serious. But whereas the Ancients regarded love, union, and offspring as of serious importance because of their role in continuing an ancestral line and maintaining family and civic traditions, Shaw regarded sex as serious because it was the chief agent of the Life Force in the process of creative evolution which made the son intellectually and emotionally superior to his father. And whereas the Ancients treated sex seriously because they respected their ancestors, Shaw treats sex seriously because he has hope in his posterity.

Shaw's reference to his own early novel, *The Irrational Knot*, contains a good description of the Life Force: "I seriously suggest that The Irrational Knot may be regarded as an early attempt on the part of the Life Force to write A Doll's House in English by the instrumentality of a very immature writer aged 24. And though I say it that should not, the choice was not such a bad shot for a stupid instinctive force that has to work and become conscious of itself by means of human brains" (*Prefaces*, p. 689).

Shaw the Artist

As we have seen, the ultimate function of Art for Shaw was to help the Life Force achieve its apotheosis of the human race. Art as religion, art as esthetic experience, art as social reform—all of these are media for bringing about the pure spirituality of the race, as we see it pictured in *Back to Methuselah*. In this view of the function of art, art is but one of the methods used by the Life Force. In *Man and Superman*, we see art and sex struggling to bring about the improvement of the race, and sex, since it is more unconscious and more primitive than art, wins the field. But, as we also learn from that play, the great artist tends to find total fulfillment in his art and often his sexual life is in disarray. For most of mankind, however, the Life Force works through the sexual instinct.

There is little doubt that when Shaw consciously discussed art he emphasized its didactic function. He writes in a letter: "And observe, the artistic faculty may work harder under the compulsion of the moral impulse than in freedom."[54] And, to be sure, he reveals scorn for a purely formalist approach to works of art. The idea that someone might analyze his prose style repelled him. But, as I have tried to show earlier in this chapter, we are not obliged to see his announced program as the whole truth, any more than we are obliged to take the intentions of any author as the whole meaning of his work. It is as plain as the shining of the sun that Shaw loved music and literature in his innermost being—they moved him, and had inexpressible meaning for him, and they formed a very large part of his sensuous life. And his appreciation of much art, especially music, was esthetic rather than ideological.

I emphasize this point because of the opposite emphasis by so many critics who saw him as little more than a talking machine with a tin ear. It was not until relatively recently that the tensions between reason and emotion were detected in his plays, because critics had tended to read the plays principally as programs. But the struggle between the rhetorical-operatic and the logical is now too apparent in his plays and in his whole personality to allow much currency to the old view. His criticisms of music and drama alone are sufficient to reveal a remarkable sensibility and a brilliant capacity to make purely esthetic judgments where they are needed.

In recent years Eric Bentley has done the greatest justice to Shaw as an artist. In his book on Shaw he goes beyond the customary one-sided accounts and gives us a reconciliation of opposites which is hard to brush aside:

Shaw has a secret, though an open one. It is that his famous method, his pose of arrogance, was a deliberate strategy in an utterly altruistic struggle. . . . His campaign of self-promotion was not the campaign of a clever careerist who decides to secure at once by cunning what he will never secure later by genius. Shaw had artistic genius enough, and knew it. Only he was not primarily interested in artistic genius and artistic reputation. He wanted his pen to be his sword in a struggle that was more ethical than aesthetic. . . . So he tried to put his genius at the service of his moral passion. He knew that this was to risk sacrificing altogether a high literary reputation. . . . The arrogant pose was an act of self-sacrifice. . . .

Of course he *is* a frustrated teacher to some extent. . . . But he is not a man of action at all. . . . He is an artist, and therefore, whatever his didactic urge, whatever the naturalistic ardor with which he seeks to portray the outer world, he gives expression to his own nature and tells the story of himself.[55] (228)

Chapter 3

NINETEENTH-CENTURY DRAMA

THERE SEEMS to be a universal opinion that British drama was moribund after the Restoration and dead after Sheridan—an opinion held not only by modern scholars but by nineteenth-century critics as well. Throughout his drama reviews, Shaw keeps telling us that British drama is virtually nonexistent, Archer tells us the same, and even an eminent dramatist of his day, Henry Arthur Jones, wrote essay after essay lamenting the fact that no serious drama of any consequence was produced by nineteenth-century British dramatists. In 1885, after seeing *As You Like It*, Shaw wrote to Archer: "But the decadence of the stage is awful. We have our work cut out for us, I can tell you. My opinion of Shakspere has gone up prodigiously: my opinion of Victorian stage culture is below zero."[1]

The explanation of this state of affairs is generally agreed upon: when the lower classes overtook the theaters in the early part of the century, the gentry retreated to the opera and to the novel, leaving drama to the vulgar. When the patent theaters of the eighteenth century were abolished as a royal institution early in the nineteenth century, new theaters of relatively immense size were built, seating as many as three thousand spectators. This impractical size, with the addition of the versatility of gas lighting, invited a spectacular drama, which usurped the stage for most of the century. Rowell describes the consequences:

The rowdy, illiterate new audiences crowded into the theatres, requiring their interest to be roused by vigorous action, their emotions moved by pathos, and their troubles soothed by a happy ending. These demands had to be met as best they could. Forced to reject much of the Georgian repertory, the new theatre found itself without a drama and had too often to substitute spectacle. In these hand-to-mouth conditions manager, actor, and author were content if the fancy of their public was caught and briefly held by a new offering. There was no time or occasion to question the standards of that offering.[2]

The modes of acting, as well as the type of drama to be performed, were affected by these demands—actors like Kean, for example, specializing in the grand, flamboyant manner. Indeed, by the time of Irving, during the last quarter of the century, delicate and exquisite attention to detail was regarded as a novelty.

By mid-century, two other influences besides spectacle predominated in the theater: the Robertsonian revolution and the well-made play. It is against these three that Shaw reacted in the nineties and in relation to these his criticism is more understandable. In 1883, when the spectacular element still prevailed, Henry Arthur Jones observed: "Thus, on inquiring why we have no national drama at all worthy of the name, we are met first of all by the fact that the drama is not merely an *art* but a *popular amusement*, in a different sense from that in which poetry, music, and painting are popular amusements. The drama is an art, but it is also a competitor of music-halls, circuses, Madame Tussaud's, the Westminster Aquarium, and the Argyll Rooms."[3] More recently, Martin Meisel has written:

In the theater of Barry Sullivan, opera and drama were much closer to each other than they are today. The two forms supplied each other with conventions and materials, and the playhouse was the opera house. The attitude of the audience for both forms was very like that of a modern opera audience; for in a day of permanent companies, great touring stars, and a familiar grand repertory, the audience judged not the play but the performance. They expressed instant approval and disapproval, waited expectantly for the virtuoso bits, and, when particularly pleased, stopped the performance and demanded the same aria or the same bravura passage over again. The actors also moved more freely between opera and drama. Barry Sullivan, Shaw's favorite among all actors, sang in opera at the beginning of his career, and Shaw classed his kind of acting with Chaliapin's. On the London stage, the gap between opera and drama widened more rapidly than in the provinces. Consequently Shaw's experience in Dublin of a more intimately related opera and drama had great importance for his later critical thinking, and ultimately for his playwriting.[4]

The plays of Tom Robertson, especially *Caste*, were a second source of major currents in mid-century drama. Robertson turned his back on rhetoric and flamboyance and devoted himself to the improvement of stage technique and the composition of relatively natural dialogue. What resulted was the Cup and Saucer drama, as it has come to be called, in which verisimilitude was achieved through the use of real props, such as doorknobs on the doors. This was the beginning of the inevitable excesses which result from emancipation from old limitations, so that Shaw was able to make fun of the fact that the audience was greatly excited by the use of real water in one of the plays he witnessed while reviewing for the *Saturday Review*. Robertson, however, did not introduce realistic details into his plays merely to create sensation. He "regularly employs a piece of stage business to catch and hold a delicate emotion which dialogue alone could not convey."[5] Thus, besides the use of real doorknobs, we find a considerable increase in non-verbal means of expression in the Robertson plays. In *Caste*, for instance, there is a famous scene involving the pouring of tea. And Rowell cites the stage direction in *The M.P.*, when the bankrupt nobleman witnesses the sale of his mother's portrait: "The actor playing Dunscombe is requested not to make too much of this situation. All that is required is a momentary memory of childhood —succeeded by the external phlegm of the man of the world. No tragedy, no tears, or pocket-handkerchief."[6] Even Shaw appreciated the increased realism and subtlety which were the result of Robertson's reform of the stage. "I do not say that the stage drawing rooms . . . were better than 'four boards and a passion'; but they were worlds above flats, wings, sky borders and no passion" (I, 277). Shaw was not blind to the advantages as well as the disadvantages of stage realism. Although he deplored the belief that the use of walls, doors, fashionable tailoring, and colloquial speech could produce a great drama in themselves (III, 152), and although he objected to the frequent sentimentality of the Robertson plays, with its "sloppy insistence on the soft place that is to be found in everybody" (III, 168), he nevertheless could remark:

After years of sham heroics and superhuman balder-dash, Caste delighted everyone by its freshness, its nature, its humanity. You will shriek and snort, O scornful young men, at this monstrous assertion. "Nature! Freshness!" you will exclaim. "In Heaven's name [if you are not too modern to have heard of Heaven],* where is there a touch of nature in Caste?" I reply, "In the windows, in the doors, in the walls, in the carpet, in the ceiling, in the kettle, in the fireplace, in the ham, in the tea, in the bread and butter, in the bassinet, in the hats and sticks and clothes, in the familiar phrases, the quiet, unpumped, everyday utterance: in short, the commonplaces that are now spurned because they are commonplaces, and were then inexpressibly welcome because they were the most unexpected of novelties. (III, 166)

Shaw even praises the characters of the play, Gerridge, Polly, Hawtree—for it *is* a charming play. But when he complained about real water, his complaint was that real water is not enough, and there were countless plays which had nothing more to offer than real water.

The third element of the drama of mid-century was "construction." This was the distinguishing mark of the *pièce bien faite*, the well-made play, perhaps more the accomplishment of Eugene Scribe than anyone else. What Scribe had done was to combine in one play all of the devices for achieving excitement which had been used separately or in limited combinations in the drama from the Greeks to the end of the eighteenth century. By the time Scribe had written a

---

* Shaw's brackets.

staggering number of plays, a clear formula emerged for the composition of a well-made play, a formula roughly like the following:[7]

The play begins with the introduction of characters who, by means of exposition, supply the audience with the information necessary to understanding what follows. Usually, the principal characters are a hero, sometimes with a friend or servant who aids him in his trials, and the opponent of the hero. Often, in place of the opponent there are a younger and an older woman, the younger somewhat naïve and pretty and the older charming and worldly. The hero is eager to marry the young woman but is opposed by the older woman, who, like Strauss's Marschallin, is forced to give him up at the end. The substance of the play is a series of crises which alternately leave the hero and his opponent victorious. There is usually a *peripeteia*, in which the hero suffers a reversal and temporary fall, often followed by a similar fall for the opponent. Later, there is inevitably a *scène à faire*, that is, an obligatory scene, in which the opponent suffers a great defeat when some dark secret is revealed detrimental to his cause. This is then followed by a recognition scene, which clears up the remaining obscurities in the plot by means of unmaskings and explanations, and, last of all, a denouement which apportions the final rewards and punishments to the main characters. Besides these conventional stages in the development of the plot, other tricks, such as the *quiproquo*, in which two characters misinterpret a word or situation but suppose they both understand it correctly, are inevitably sprinkled throughout the play.

Stephen Stanton points out that many plays contain one or more of these devices but that they cannot be considered well-made unless they make use of virtually all of them and in the correct order. With construction emphasized over theme and character, what was produced was a masterpiece of suspenseful excitement. A well-made play can hardly avoid being a great popular success, for we may recall E. M. Forster's observation that the most primitive desire in an audience is the desire to know what happens next. If we examine a well-made play like Scribe's *The Glass of Water*, we find a series of situations and reversals (as in the plays of Beaumont and Fletcher) of the most exciting character imaginable. Furthermore, since Scribe had wit, the play is delightful in addition to being exciting.

Scribe is quoted as saying: "You go to the theatre for relaxation and amusement, not for instruction or correction. Now what most amuses you is not truth but fiction. . . . The theatre is therefore rarely the direct expression of social life . . . it is often the inverse expression."[8] We can see at once that Shaw would violently reject such a notion, which in a Shavian universe is absolutely immoral. But the amusing irony with regard to well-made plays is that both Ibsen and Shaw wrote them. If Sardou used his powers of construction in order to write plays which were illogical and a bit mad, Dumas and Augier used the Scribean tricks in order to write social drama—and so did Ibsen, Wilde, and Shaw himself. If Scribe "is to be damned for the prattle of Sardou he may as well be canonized for the thunder of Ibsen; the dramaturgy is basically pretty much the same."[9] Stephen Stanton notes that since Scribe's great contribution to the art of construction was the use of logic and probability, the Scribean well-made play was well suited to the needs of the nineteenth-century problem play, which did not emerge in England until the second half of the century.

Out of the theatrical devices that yielded the thin but amusing characterizations of Scribe the author of *Arms and the Man* developed three-dimensional persons.

The well-made play, then, was serviceable to two kinds of British dramatist: the kind that wanted nothing but to exploit the proved methods of one of the most commercially successful playwrights in history, and the kind that saw how a deadly satire of Victorian complacency could be devised from the inversion of these methods. If Wilde and Shaw wrote masterpieces whereas Pinero, except for one or two superior achievements, remained a mediocrity, the difference is a tribute to the genius of Wilde and Shaw. They borrowed their theatrical tricks, as Pinero borrowed his, from Scribe, French boulevard farce, and Adelphi melodrama; but out of them they managed to create refreshing and provocative examples of dramatic art.[10]

Although superior dramatists like Wilde and Shaw were able to make special use of French techniques, earlier dramatists with no originality were content to adapt already existing French plays into English. William Archer writes: "Adaptation became the very simplest of crafts, and, for something like half a century, anyone who could buy, borrow or steal a French dictionary could set up in business as a playwright."[11] In addition to adaptations, we find that the plays of mid-century often made use of techniques of construction even when the plays were original. A popular play of its time like Boucicault's *Colleen Bawn* is a typical well-made play in Irish dress. Confused identity, mistaken interpretations, intercepted letters, overheard conversations misunderstood—the play is built entirely of these devices. And again, later in the century, the plays of Sydney Grundy were built from the thin moral overtones and thick constructions of French originals.

Shaw objected strongly to the assumptions and methods of French construction. He did not believe that the purpose of the theater was merely to amuse; he did not believe that plot was important. Furthermore, since the well-made play leaves little room for creation of character or sufficiently developed speeches, Shaw found the genre sterile and useless:

How to Write a Popular Play

The formula for the well made play is so easy that I give it for the benefit of any reader who feels tempted to try his hand at making the fortune that awaits all successful manufacturers in this line. First, you "have an idea" for a dramatic situation. If it strikes you as a splendidly original idea whilst it is in fact as old as the hills, so much the better. For instance, the situation of an innocent person convicted by circumstances of a crime may always be depended on. If the person is a woman, she must be convicted of adultery. If a young officer, he must be convicted of selling information to the enemy . . . . Comedy is more difficult . . . but the process is essentially the same: it is the manufacture of a misunderstanding. Having manufactured it, you place its culmination at the end of the last act but one, which is the point at which the manufacture of the play begins. Then you make your first act out of the necessary introduction of the characters to the audience, after elaborate explanations, mostly conducted by servants, solicitors, and other low life personages (the principals must all be dukes and colonels and millionaires), of how the misunderstanding is going to come about. Your last act consists, of course, of clearing up the misunderstanding, and generally getting the audience out of the theatre as best you can. (*Prefaces*, p. 203)

Of course, even the writer of a well-made play must have some talent, for sheer mechanics are not enough. But, Shaw wants to know, why write a constructed play in the first place when so many more profound matters are ready to hand? How tiresome is exposition in the first act, situation in the second, and denouement in the third! Shaw admitted that even Ibsen at first wrote plays in the French manner, but in those he at least substituted a discussion in act three for the unraveling (*Essays*, p. 135).

Some of Shaw's most scintillating reviews were provoked by the clockworks of Sardou. Of *Delia Harding*, he wrote:

Delia Harding is the worst play I ever saw. . . . Sardou's plan of playwriting is first to invent the action of his piece, and then to carefully keep it off the stage and have it announced merely by letters and telegrams. The people open the letters and read them, whether they are addressed to them or not; and then they talk either about what the letters announce as having occurred already or about what they intend to do tomorrow in consequence of receiving them. When the news is not brought by post, the characters are pressed into the service. Delia Harding, for instance, consists largely of the fashionable intelligence in Bellagio. As thus: "Stanley French arrived in Bellagio this morning," "Mr Harding will arrive in Bellagio tomorrow afternoon," "Miss Harding lives in that villa on the lake," "Sir Christopher Carstairs will remain here for another month at least," "This is my brother, Sir Arthur Studley," "Janet: we shall pack up and leave tomorrow morning," etc. etc., the person addressed invariably

74

echoing with subdued horror, "This morning!" "To-morrow afternoon!" "In *that* villa!" and so on. (I, 97-98)

The famous review of *Fedora*, entitled "Sardoodle-dom," commences: "Up to this day week I had pre-served my innocence as a playgoer sufficiently never to have seen Fedora. Of course I was not altogether new to it, since I had seen Diplomacy Dora, and Theodora, and La Toscadora, and other machine dolls from the same firm. And yet the thing took me aback" (I, 133). Shaw then complains of all the dull machinery, the letters, telegrams, timetables, arrivals, and departures. In his review of Sardou's *Gismonda*, he observes: "The scene being laid in the Middle Ages, there are no news-papers, letters, or telegrams; but this is far from being an advantage, as the characters tell each other the news all through except when a child is dropped into a tiger's cage as a cue for Madame Bernhardt's popular scream" (I, 137).

Long after his *Saturday Review* days, looking back on the plays he used to review, and at his own plays, Shaw remarked that, to critics used to the adulteries and duels of the French stage, his own plays seemed like "pamphlets in dialogue."[12] "Bored by the artificial 'constructions' which supplanted genuine classic drama on the Parisian stage in the nineteenth century . . . [I] went back to Shakespear, and finally even to the Athen-ian theatre with its unities of time and place."[13] Shaw believed that a serious play had to grow organically from a germinal idea in the author's mind, whereas a "constructed" play needed no ideas—merely crises. "A play is a vital growth and not a mechanical construction . . . a plot is the ruin of a story and therefore of a play, which is essentially a story." A good play will "construct itself, like a flowering plant, far more wonderfully than its author can consciously construct it" (*Pen Portraits*, p. 22). Even William Archer, in 1897, asked: "Has Eugène Scribe spoken the last word of theatrical technique? . . . Has not his art, which, in its novelty, was immensely interesting and attractive, come to seem, through sheer familiarity, a somewhat tedious artifice? Is there not an art beyond his art, an art which conceals art, a higher skill which minimises the mechanical element in drama, and so leaves more room for character, thought, emotion, humour, the essential components of life?"[14]

Although the well-made play had had its most flourishing life during the years before Shaw was a reviewer, the techniques of construction which characterize it were still in widespread use in the nineties. Shaw never missed an opportunity to reveal and satirize transparent mechanical tricks in the plays he reviewed. The very first play which he attended after having been hired by the *Saturday Review* was Grundy's *Slaves of the Ring*. Grundy, specializing in well-made plays, was the first dramatist to be immortalized by Shavian desecrations in *Our Theatres in the Nineties*. When Grundy makes his characters slap each other's faces with gloves, "it is really impossible to do anything but laugh and fish out one's hat to go" (I, 4); his constructions are transparent: ". . . he owes it to his reputation as a master of stage technique that she [a female character in the play] should announce her presence by turning up a lamp, which the other lady has previously had turned down for that express purpose (as every experienced playgoer in the house plainly foresees) on the somewhat emaciated pretext that she prefers to sit in the dark" (I, 2). In addition, Grundy was addicted to the interminable expositions of prior circumstances which are necessary to get the well-made play under way: "The third act was better. There were no explanations, because, the murder being out, there was nothing more to explain. Unfortunately, though the plot was over, it was too late to begin the play. Further, the scene was in a conservatory, lit with so many lamps that Miss Rorke could not have made any particular difference by turning down one of them" (I, 4). This is what happens when the author's imagination is "stretched and tortured . . . on the Procrustean framework of 'the well-made play'" (I, 4).

No device borrowed from Scribe offended Shaw more than his method of exposition. He complains of the inevitable two servants who enter to gossip about their employers' affairs (II, 149), and he explains that it is the second-rate dramatist who begins his play with explanations before he can get the action under way. The first-rate dramatist begins in the middle of the action, and Ibsen begins at the end (II, 84). Shaw was particularly severe against Pinero, doubtless because of the praise which Pinero received from other quarters. In the first act of *The Second Mrs. Tanqueray*, Cayley Drummle goes offstage to write letters in order to permit the onstage characters to talk about him. Shaw laughed at

. . . the naïve machinery of the exposition of the first act, in which two whole actors are wasted on sham parts, and the hero, at his own dinner party, is compelled to get up and go ignominiously into the next room "to write some letters" when something has to be said behind his back; when one follows Cayley Drummle, the confidant to whom both Paula and her husband explain themselves for the benefit of the audience; when one counts the number of doors which Mr Pinero needs to get his characters on and off the stage, and how they have finally to be supplemented by the inevitable "French windows" (two of them); and when the activity of the postman is taken into consideration, it is impossible to avoid the conclusion that what most of our critics mean by mastery of stage craft is recklessness in the substitution of dead machinery and lay figures for vital action and real characters. (I, 45-46)

This attack on Pinero's craftsmanship is just one of the many instances in which Shaw displayed much keener perception of the real substance of Pinero's dramas than most of the other critics. For the other critics were taken in by the superficially striking novelties of *The Second Mrs. Tanqueray.*

When *The Notorious Mrs. Ebbsmith*, another Pinero success, made its debut in March, 1895, Shaw complained of the tediousness of the first twenty minutes, "with its intolerable, unnecessary, and unintelligible explanations about the relationships of the characters" (I, 64), which he said he did not listen to anyhow. And when he went to see the play a second time he made certain to come late enough to miss the explanations altogether (I, 126).

Spectacle, construction, and real doorknobs: these, then, were features of much nineteenth-century drama. Late in the century a fourth element began to gain a place in a substantial minority of plays: the problem. The problem, above all, served Shaw's own turn and enabled him to emerge alone distinguished from the mass of Victorian playwrights. But recognition of Shaw's distinction was quite late, not until a decade of the twentieth century had elapsed, whereas the real hero of the nineties, the acclaimed daring innovator, was Pinero. The irony of the rise of Pinero, however, was that while the critics were acclaiming Pinero as a vital new force capable of reviving British drama, Shaw was making fun of him, and even though Shaw was harshly taxed for not appreciating Pinero's genius, taxed even by his friend Archer, his penetrating judgment and almost unerring taste enabled him not only to give a truly just estimate of Pinero's powers but to become Pinero's successor.

Pinero's career as a dramatist began in the late 1870's and was influenced by both Robertson and the well-made play.[15] From the beginning he demonstrated a versatility in genre which lasted through his productive years. Three of his earlier plays—*Imprudence, The Money-Spinner,* and *The Squire*—were respectively farce, melodrama, and problem play, which were to be his major forms. Pinero learned a good deal about construction as a result of his adaptations from the French, and he used this knowledge to advantage in some of his farces of the 1880's, like *The Magistrate, The Schoolmistress,* and *Dandy Dick.* Rowell finds, even in these early pieces, hints of Pinero's predilection for serious problems, which finally exploded in *The Profligate* with such suddenness that Pinero was forced to make changes in the play to suit it for popular consumption before its first performance. Not long after this play, he produced *The Second Mrs. Tanqueray,* which was to make his reputation as a serious dramatist.

It is hard to read Pinero's two great successes, *The Second Mrs. Tanqueray* and *The Notorious Mrs. Ebbsmith,* and see exactly what excited people in the nineties. Shaw saw, almost at once, what to us must now appear glaring defects. Under the pretence of being problem plays, *The Second Mrs. Tanqueray* and *The Notorious Mrs. Ebbsmith* were in actuality well-made plays which offered the flavor of thought but which had no sensible thought to offer. Melodrama, unbelievable changes in the fortunes of the protagonists, clumsy stage machinery, unreal characters, tedious expositions, and an irresponsible use of "problems" instead of actions to achieve excitement—these are the major defects of the Pinero plays. What is most offensive, and what irritated Shaw the most, was that the plays dealt with social issues in a manner serious enough not to be comedy or burlesque, but superficial enough to keep the tension mounting without making any penetrating, or even commonsensical, observations about the problems. Mrs. Ebbsmith's numerous reversals are nothing more than a modern version of *The Maid's Tragedy*, with love replaced as the main subject by a combination of sex and "social problem." Instead of a love story about a woman of rank, we have one about a woman interested in street-corner politicking. The result is a good deal of nonsense about the nature of women, hardly more "advanced" than "a woman's place is in the home." However, when the excitement is over (and it is handled in the best Scribean manner, but with ideas replacing actions), one cannot be sure what all the fuss has been about.

Fittingly enough, to Shaw the radical Pinero was really a reactionary: "It is Mr Pinero's confounded aptitude for doing what other people have done before that makes him a reactionary force in English dramatic literature, and helps to keep the stage bound to the follies of the eighteen-sixties" (III, 347). "It seems to me that the world is to him still the world of . . . Vincent Crummles and Newman Noggs: his Paula Tanquerays and Mrs Ebbsmiths appearing as pure aberrations whose external differences he is able to observe as far as they can be observed without the inner clue, but whose point of view he has never found" (III, 309). The reason for this, said Shaw, was that Pinero did not have intellectual views at all, that his world of "problems" and his characters were entirely fictitious in the sense of having very little relation to anything but a theatrical reality. He is a gentleman: "I will shew just enough of your weaknesses to make you interesting" is his offer (III, 93), but not enough to make you understandable, one could add. Shaw continues the little speech he puts into Pinero's mouth by having him remark: "I have no convictions, no views, no general ideas of any kind: I am simply a dramatic artist, only too glad to accept a point of view" which will make characters appealing (III, 94).

The Second Mrs. Tanqueray, which Stephen Stanton regards as modeled after Augier's Olympia's Marriage (and which confirms one's suspicions of its well-made-ness) and Scribe in general, is possibly the play which Shaw refers to more than any outside of Ibsen. For Mrs. Tanqueray was a tease who deluded the public into thinking that the British theater had finally obtained what it needed: a profound and searching school of drama dealing with real problems. That the public believed they had obtained such a school was enough to make Shaw doubly furious with Pinero. Unfortunately, the play originally appeared before Shaw's reviews began, so that what we have are not Shaw's first reactions. But we have enough. When Shaw was able to praise a late comedy by Pinero, in 1895, he contrasted its genuine talents with the specious ones of Tanqueray. Pinero, he writes, maintained it at an astonishingly high and even pressure for two hours, without for a moment being driven back on the woman with a past, the cynical libertine peer, the angel of purity, the Cayley Drummle confidant, or any other of the conventional figures which inevitably appear in his plays whenever he conceives himself to be dealing as a sociologist with public questions of which he has no solid knowledge, but only a purely conventional and theatrical conceit. . . . Mr Pinero has not exactly been born again—but at least there are no intercepted letters, or sendings of one set of people to France and another to India in order to enable a lady to arrive unexpectedly or a gentleman to walk in by night at the drawing room window. (I, 217-18)

When *The Second Mrs. Tanqueray* was published, in 1895, Shaw felt that its real defects became all the more apparent in print. On the stage Paula Tanqueray was relatively well drawn for her day, but on the page she showed Pinero to be a disciple of the nineteenth-century novel—of Bulwer-Lytton, Reade, and Trollope. He "has never written a line from which it could be guessed that he is a contemporary of Ibsen, Tolstoi, Meredith, or Sarah Grand" (I, 45).

The effect of Mrs. Tanqueray on the theatrical world of her day was very great. Indeed, when Reginald Golding Bright, Shaw's young correspondent, refers in passing to "the sublime tragedy of Mrs. Tanqueray," Shaw crosses out the remark and pleads, "No, Reginald, no. Not again."[16] "Mrs. Tanqueray is your Dulcinea; and you will never be worth a guinea a column until you grow out of her."[17]

The Notorious Mrs. Ebbsmith appeared on the stage for the first time in March, 1895. Since the play occasioned the most brilliant essay among his dramatic reviews, and since the analysis of "Pinerotic" drama is definitive, I reproduce Shaw's review entire:

Mr Pinero's new play is an attempt to reproduce that peculiar stage effect of intellectual drama, of social problem, of subtle psychological study of character, in short, of a great play, with which he was so successful in The Profligate and The Second Mrs Tanqueray. In the two earlier plays, it will be remembered, he was careful to support this stage effect with a substantial basis of ordinary dramatic material, consisting of a well worked-up and well worn situation which would have secured the success of a conventional Adelphi piece. In this way he conquered the public by the exquisite flattery of giving them plays that they really liked, whilst persuading them that such appreciation was only possible from persons of great culture and intellectual acuteness. The vogue of The Second Mrs Tanqueray was due to the fact that the commonplace playgoer, as he admired Mrs Patrick Campbell, and was moved for the twentieth time by the conventional wicked woman with a past, consumed with remorse at the recollection of her innocent girlhood, and unable to look her pure step-daughter (from a convent) in the face, believed that he was one of the select few for whom "the literary drama" exists, and thus combined the delights of an evening at a play which would not have puzzled Madame Celeste with a sense of being immensely in the modern movement. Mr Pinero, in effect, invented a new sort of play by taking the ordinary article and giving it an air of novel, profound, and original thought. This he was able to do because he was an inveterate "character actor" (a technical term denoting a clever stage performer who cannot act, and therefore makes an elaborate study of the disguises and stage tricks by which acting can be grotesquely simulated) as well as a competent dramatist on customary lines. His performance as a thinker and social philosopher is simply character acting in the domain of authorship, and can impose only on those who are taken in by character acting on the stage. It is only the make-up of an actor who does not understand his part, but who knows—because he shares—the popular notion of its externals. As such, it can never be the governing factor in his success, which must always depend on the commonplace but real substratum of ordinary drama in his works. Thus his power to provide Mrs Tanqueray with equally popular successors depends on his freedom from the illusion he has himself created as to his real strength lying in his acuteness as a critic of life. Given a good play, the stage effect of philosophy will pass with those who are no better philosophers than he; but when the play is bad, the air of philosophy can only add to its insufferableness. In the case of The Notorious Mrs. Ebbsmith, the play is bad. But one of its defects: to wit, the unreality of the chief female character, who is fully as artificial as Mrs Tanqueray herself, has the lucky effect of setting Mrs Patrick Campbell free to do as she pleases in it, the result being an irresistible projection of that lady's personal genius, a projection which sweeps the play aside and imperiously becomes the play itself. Mrs Patrick Campbell, in fact, pulls her author through by playing him clean off the stage. She creates all sorts of illusions, and gives one all sorts of searching sensations. It is impossible not to feel that those haunting eyes are brooding on a momentous past, and the parted lips anticipating a thrilling imminent future, whilst some enigmatic present must no less surely be working underneath all that subtle play of limb and stealthy intensity of tone. Clearly there must be a great tragedy somewhere in the immediate neighborhood; and most of my colleagues will no doubt tell us that this imaginary masterpiece is Mr Pinero's Notorious Mrs Ebbsmith. But Mr Pinero has hardly anything to do with it. When the curtain comes down, you are compelled to admit that, after all, nothing has come of it except your conviction that Mrs Patrick Campbell is a wonderful woman. Let us put her out of the question for a moment and take a look at Mrs Ebbsmith.

To begin with, she is what has been called "a platform woman." She is the daughter of a secularist agitator—say a minor Bradlaugh. After eight years of married life, during which she was for one year her husband's sultana, and for the other seven his housekeeper, she has emerged into widowhood and an active career as an agitator, speaking from the platforms formerly occupied by her father. Although educated, well conducted, beautiful, and a sufficiently powerful speaker to produce a great effect in Trafalgar Square, she loses her voice from starvation, and has to fall back on nursing—a piece of fiction which shews that Mr Pinero has not the faintest idea of what such a woman's career is in reality. He may take my word for it that a lady with such qualification would be very much better off than a nurse; and that the plinth of the Nelson column, the "pitch" in the park, and the little meeting halls in poor parishes, all of which he speaks of with such an exquisitely suburban sense of their being the dark places of the earth, enter nowadays very largely into the political education of almost all publicly active men and women; so that the Duke of St Olpherts, when he went to that iron building in St Luke's, and saw "Mad Agnes" on the platform, might much more probably have found there a future Cabinet Minister, a lady of his own ducal family, or even a dramatic critic. However, the mistakes into which Mr Pinero has been led by his want of practical acquaintance with the business of political agitation are of no great dramatic moment. We may forgive a modern British dramatist for supposing that Mrs Besant, for example, was an outcast on the brink of starvation in the days when she graduated on the platform, although we should certainly not tolerate such nonsense from any intellectually responsible person. But Mr Pinero has made a deeper mistake. He has fallen into the common error of supposing that the woman who speaks in public and takes an interest in wider concerns than those of her own household is a special variety of the human species; that she "Trafalgar Squares" aristocratic visitors in her drawing room; and that there is something dramatic in her discovery that she has the common passions of humanity.

Mrs Ebbsmith, in the course of her nursing, finds a patient who falls in love with her. He is married to a shrew; and he proposes to spend the rest of his life with his nurse, preaching the horrors of marriage. Off the stage it is not customary for a man and woman to assume that they cannot co-operate in bringing about social reform without living together as man and wife: on the stage, this is considered inevitable. Mrs Ebbsmith rebels against the stage so far as to propose that they shall prove their disinterestedness by making the partnership a friendly business one only. She then finds that he does not really care a rap about her ideas, and that his attachment to her is simply sexual. Here we start with a dramatic theme capable of interesting development. Mr Pinero, unable to develop it, lets it slip through his fingers after one feeble clutch at it, and proceeds to degrade his drama below the ordinary level by making the woman declare that her discovery of the nature of the man's feelings put within her reach "the only one hour in a woman's life," in pursuance of which detestable view she puts on an indecent dress and utterly abandons herself to him. A clergyman appears at this crisis, and offers her a Bible. She promptly pitches it into the stove; and a thrill of horror runs through the audience as they see, in imagination, the whole Christian Church tottering before their eyes. Suddenly, with a wild scream, she plunges her hand into the glowing stove and pulls out the Bible again. The Church is saved; and the curtain descends amid thunders of applause. In that applause I hope I need not say I did not join. A less sensible and less courageous stage effect I have never witnessed. If Mr Pinero had created for us a woman whose childhood had been made miserable by the gloomy terrorism which vulgar, fanatical parents extract from the Bible, then he might fitly have given some of the public a very wholesome lesson by making the woman thrust the Bible into the stove and leave it there. Many of the most devoted clergymen of the Church of England would, I can assure him, have publicly thanked him for such a lesson. But to introduce a woman as to whom we are carefully assured that she was educated as a secularist, and whose one misfortune—her unhappy marriage—can hardly by any stretch of casuistry be laid to the charge of St Paul's teaching; to make this woman senselessly say that all her misfortunes are due to the Bible; to make her throw it into the stove, and then injure herself horribly in pulling it out again: this, I submit, is a piece of claptrap so gross that it absolves me from all obligations to treat Mr Pinero's art as anything higher than the barest art of theatrical sensation. As in The Profligate, as in The Second Mrs Tanqueray, he has had no idea beyond that of doing something daring and bringing down the house by running away from the consequences.

I must confess that I have no criticism for all this

stuff. Mr Pinero is quite right to try his hand at the higher drama; only he will never succeed on his present method of trusting to his imagination, which seems to me to have been fed originally on the novels and American humor of forty years ago, and of late to have been entirely starved. I strongly recommend him to air his ideas a little in Hyde Park or "the Iron Hall, St Luke's," before he writes his next play. I shall be happy to take the chair for him.

I should, by the way, like to know the truth about the great stage effect at the end of the second act, where Mrs Patrick Campbell enters with her plain and very becoming dress changed for a horrifying confection apparently made of Japanese bronze wall-paper with a bold pattern of stamped gold. Lest the maker should take an action against me and obtain ruinous damages, I hasten to say that the garment was well made, the skirt and train perfectly hung, and the bodice, or rather waistband, fitting flawlessly. But, as I know nothing of the fashion in evening dresses, it was cut rather lower in the pectoral region than I expected; and it was, to my taste, appallingly ugly. So I fully believed that the effect intended was a terrible rebuke to the man's complaint that Mrs Ebbsmith's previous dress was only fit for "a dowdy demagogue." Conceive my feelings when everyone on the stage went into ecstasies of admiration. Can Mr Pinero have shared that admiration? As the hero of a recent play observes, "That is the question that torments me."

A great deal of the performance is extremely tedious. The first twenty minutes, with its intolerable, unnecessary, and unintelligible explanations about the relationships of the characters, should be ruthlessly cut out. Half the stage business is only Mr Pinero's old "character actor" nonsense; and much of the other half might be executed during the dialogue, and not be-

tween the sentences. The company need to be re-
minded that the Garrick is a theatre in which very
distinct utterance is desirable. The worrying from time
to time about the stove should be dropped, as it does
not in the least fulfil its purpose of making the Bible
incident—which is badly stage managed—seem more
natural when it comes.

Mr Hare, in the stalest of parts, gives us a perfect
piece of acting, not only executed with extraordinary
fineness, but conceived so as to produce a strong illusion that there is a real character there, whereas there
is really nothing but that hackneyed simulacrum of a
cynical and epigrammatic old libertine who has helped
to carry on so many plots. Mr Forbes Robertson lent
himself to the hero, and so enabled him to become
interesting on credit. Miss Jeffreys, miraculously ill
fiitted with her part, was pleasant for the first five min-
uates, during which she was suggesting a perfectly different sort of person to that which she afterwards vainly
pretended to become. The other characters were the
merest stock figures, convincing us that Mr Pinero
either never meets anybody now, or else that he has
lost the power of observation. Many passages in the
play, of course, have all the qualities which have gained
Mr Pinero his position as a dramatist; but I shall not
dwell on them, as, to tell the truth, I disliked the play
so much that nothing would induce me to say anything
good of it. And here let me warn the reader to carefully
discount my opinion in view of the fact that I write
plays myself, and that my school is in violent reaction
against that of Mr Pinero. But my criticism has not, I
hope, any other fault than the inevitable one of extreme unfairness. (I, 59-65)

Despite the outrageousness of Shaw's treatment of the
play, his review cannot be said to distort or misrepre-
sent the artistic pretensions of The Notorious Mrs.

Ebbsmith. As if such a review were not enough, there is a postscript only two months later, when Shaw went to see the play again:

By the way, I have received a sixpenny pamphlet by Mr H. Schütz Wilson, entitled The Notorious Mrs Ebbsmith, published by Messrs Bickers. My opinion being thus challenged, I cheerfully acknowledge the pre-eminence of the pamphlet, from my point of view, as the worst pamphlet I ever read on any subject whatsoever. That, however, is only a way of saying that I cannot agree with Mr Schütz Wilson. The difference may be my fault as well as my misfortune. He accepts the play as a great "spiritual tragedy," and considers that the casting of it at the Garrick Theatre was perfect in every part. And so, as he says, "Farewell, Agnes! and may all good go with you in the future. After all, you did not burn THE BOOK." (I, 129)

In one of his letters, Shaw wrote: "A man who, at Pinero's age and in his position and with his secure bank account, could bring himself to that Bible business, is hopelessly damned."[18] Although it is easy to laugh off Mr. Schütz Wilson, one is less delighted when the eulogies come from William Archer. Shaw, seer as he was, knew Archer's limitations well—and even prefaced a book of Archer's plays with an introduction which was impartial in its praise and blame:

The theatre was not to him a workshop but part of his fairyland. He never really got behind the scenes, and never wanted to. The illusion that had charmed his youth was so strong and lasting that not even fifty years of professional theatre-going in London could dispel it. Inevitably then he liked the theatre as he found it at first: the theatre of the French "well-made play." (*Pen Portraits*, p. 18)

He did not agree with me that the form of drama which had been perfected in the middle of the nineteenth century in the French theatre was essentially mechanistic and therefore incapable of producing vital drama. That it was exhausted and, for the moment, sterile, was too obvious to escape an observer of his intelligence; but he saw nothing fundamentally wrong with it, and to the end of his life maintained that it was indispensable as a form for sound theatrical work, needing only to be brought into contact with life by having new ideas poured into it. (*Pen Portraits*, p. 22)

And in a letter to Archer, Shaw advised, "Unless you take your part in the production of the 'new drama,' you will be driven . . . to abuse it frantically, and to champion the reactionary drama against it."[19]

In 1895, Archer reviewed *The Notorious Mrs. Ebbsmith*, but his conclusions about Pinero's artistic ability are not those of Shaw: "For the rest," he wrote, "*The Notorious Mrs. Ebbsmith* seems to me the work of a born and highly accomplished dramatist, who goes right essentially and by instinct, and wrong superficially, for lack of special knowledge."[20] In his book on British drama, written in the 1920's, Archer admitted that Pinero had perhaps been overpraised and overblamed. "I myself was, I suppose, among the overpraisers; but, if so, my part was much more honourable than that of the stone-throwers."[21] Shaw, of course, he regards as among the worst of the stone-throwers, finding particularly objectionable Shaw's doctrine of predestination as applied to the character of Paula Tanqueray. Shaw had said that he was sure she was already the same at three as she was at thirty-three—that is, licentious. Although Archer found this intolerable, it is the very foundation of Shavian drama. "I perceive,"

Shaw has remarked, "the value and truth of Calvin's conviction that once a man is born it is too late to save him or damn him: you may 'educate' him and 'form his character' until you are black in the face; he is predestinate, and his soul cannot be changed any more than a silk purse can be changed into a sow's ear" (*Pen Portraits*, p. 87).

In 1932, Archibald Henderson summed up the Shaw-Archer estimations of Pinero: "It is clear today, in the light of Archer's ludicrous panegyrics of Pinero and step-motherly depreciation of Shaw, of Pinero's deliberate sacrifice of his Tanquerayan glitter to moral earnestness in the admirable serious plays of his 'third manner,' and of Shaw's advance to the zenith of world-fame as dramatist, how wrong and myopic were Archer and Walkley, how right if irritating was Shaw."[22] Shaw did not have occasion to praise Pinero until his comedy, *The Benefit of the Doubt*, was performed, at which time Shaw attributed Pinero's improvement to reading his unfavorable reviews of Pinero's previous "serious" plays. Apparently Shaw's basic kindness inclined him to try to make amends, for he teases Pinero with charm and friendliness:

Mr Pinero, after declaring that for a fortnight after the production of one of his plays he reads nothing but The Mining Journal, proceeds as follows (I italicize the phrases on which my case is founded): "One of the flaws of my system is that it robs me of the privilege of reading *much brilliant writing*. For instance, I am compelled by my system, wholly to abstain from studying those articles upon dramatic matters contributed to a well-known journal by your friend, Mr. G***** B****** S***—*of whom I protest I am, in general, a warm admirer*." Very well then, how does he know that my writing is brilliant? How can he be a warm admirer of an author he never reads—unless his admiration is excited solely by my personal appearance? Such an affectation would not impose on a baby. Besides, look at the collateral evidence. Consider the enormous improvement which took place in his work between The Notorious Mrs Ebbsmith, written before my dramatic articles had been in currency long enough to produce any effect, and The Benefit of the Doubt, written when I had been in the field for a whole year! What other cause can be assigned for this beneficent change that was not equally operative between The Second Mrs Tanqueray and The Notorious Mrs Ebbsmith—a period of temporary decline? None—absolutely none. And yet I am to be told that Mr Pinero reads The Mining Journal instead of The Saturday Review! Stuff! Why, Mr Pinero is one of the most conspicuous of the very, very few playwrights we have who are more interested in the drama than in mines. (II, 56)

Pinero, Ibsen, and Shakespeare—these are the three main dramatists with whom Shaw concerned himself not only in his drama reviews but in the course of his whole lifetime. Pinero was, for the most part, a whipping boy. Perhaps his main defect was that he was not Ibsen and stubbornly refused to be Ibsen. But during the nineties there was no Ibsen but Ibsen himself. For a while Shaw had some hope for Henry Arthur Jones, but it was not well founded.

Jones was influenced in his early career primarily by Robertsonian drama and by melodrama. But added to these influences was a serious interest in social problems and a serious regard for the drama as art. He did as a matter of course write comedies and farces like The Deacon and The Liars, but in the preface to

Saints and Sinners, first produced in 1884, Jones revealed his desire to infuse art and philosophy into his
work. His aims and his failures are described by Nicoll:

Jones here made a plea for the introduction into the
theatre of larger problems still, of questions not concerned with man's relation to man but of those where
man's relation to God was the object of enquiry. Bold
as this endeavour was, however, Jones failed in two
ways. First of all, here as elsewhere, he was apt to inter-
pret religious problems in a material way. His interest
is not in faith and pious rapture but in sectarian conventions and the outward manifestations of piety. The beliefs of a particular church concern him little; his mind
is mightily occupied with the social results of the clash
between church and chapel. Secondly, because of his
training in melodrama, Jones constantly falsifies and
makes artificial both his situations and his characters.[23]

Jones also showed his desire to attempt greater things
than Pinero by writing verse drama such as *The
Tempter*. But his limited poetic ability and his limited
mind prevented success. What is unfortunate in the
case of Jones as a dramatist is that he was interested in
more than fame and financial success—interested in
spiritual problems and their representation in art—but
no matter how earnestly he devoted himself to the task
of producing drama worthy of the best English traditions, he could not rise above melodramatic sensation-
alism and theatrical displays. Nicoll observes that Jones
would have been very much at home in Dryden's England, turning out the heroic dramas then fashionable.

Because of the serious and devoted elements in
Jones's plays, Shaw was inclined to give Jones a good
deal of encouragement and, in fact, undeserved praise,
hoping, no doubt, to rouse him to his best work. Shaw

ascribed to him "creative imagination, curious observation, inventive humor, originality, sympathy, and sincerity" (I, 123) and claimed that his characters were passionately drawn from real life (III, 93). Jones's most ambitious play during the years Shaw wrote for the *Saturday Review—Michael and His Lost Angel—* did not substantiate Shaw's hopes. The review begins with Shaw's praise of Jones's technical skill. Shaw singles him out above Sardou, Pinero, Grundy, and the others, as a serious dramatist who is not interested in the hollow construction of the French school. He even praises the first two acts of the play. But he is disappointed at the last by Jones's lack of moral strength— which forces him into a dramatic denouement in which the main characters suffer traditionally melodramatic stage fates (entering a monastery, and dying) instead of facing up to the realities of their moral constitutions. Jones continued to let Shaw down by failing to show that strength and unity of mind which Shaw demanded in all art. Nicoll's summary of Jones as a dramatist is similar to Shaw's final evaluation. Nicoll remarks:

In a pure melodrama we do not seek for anything beyond common standards; our dissatisfaction with Jones arises from the fact that he considers himself somewhat superior to this level and consequently raises expectations which, because of his intellectual inferiority, he cannot satisfy.

So far as the new drama is concerned, Jones's contribution was therefore indirect rather than direct. He awakened the desire for something that should stimulate thought even although his own plays remained bound by a middle-class morality innocent of thought or vision.[24]

Many years later, in 1921, Shaw makes a mysterious remark which he does not amplify: "But if I pretend to think that Jones's mind is no better than three-penn'orth of cat's meat, he will dig up my old Saturday Review articles and confute me from my own pen" (*Pen Portraits*, p. 172). I think we must draw from this remark Shaw's ultimate abandonment of faith in Jones's ability and a recantation of the praises from the reviews which I have just summarized. Even though Jones was not able to fill the need of the age in practice, he did, at any rate, have an interest in dramatic theory, as can be seen from his own remarks in *The Renascence of the English Drama*:

. . . unless it is touched with this sense of eternity, wrapped round with the splendour of heroism, and imbedded in what is primary and of everlasting import, the mere reproduction on the stage of the commonplace details of everyday life must always be barren, worthless, and evanescent. Because a thing has happened in real, everyday life, is no reason for putting it on the stage. Humdrum is one of the infinities. . . . there is but one thing that is worth representing on the stage—the heart and soul, the passions and emotions of man. . . . When a dramatist has deafened and terrified us with a thousand explosions, he has done nothing; when he has surprised us with a situation, he has done nothing; when a stage-manager has marshalled his thousand supers, and drilled them into graceful attitudes and imposing processions, he has done nothing; when a scenic artist has painted for us miles upon miles of Atlantic Ocean, we are yet unsatisfied, or we should be. When a dramatist has shown us the inside of any one human heart, he has done all.[25]

Although Jones perceived the limitations of the various schools of drama then in vogue—the Robertsonian, the

Scribean, and the spectacular—he was not able to sup-
plant them with a superior.

Shaw saw his own plays as the heralds of a new dramatic age, for, as it turned out, *he* was the messiah he
had long been awaiting. He regarded *Man and Superman* as the beginning of serious intellectual drama on
the English stage (*Prefaces*, p. 546) and contrasted his
long, rhetorical speeches with the staccato sallies of the
well-made play. Looking at his own plays, he observed
that the drama moved in cycles and that he was responsible for a return to Shakespearean rhetoric and poetry:

In a generation which knew nothing of any sort of acting but drawing-room acting, and which considered a
speech of more than twenty words impossibly long, I
went back to the classical style and wrote long rhetorical speeches like operatic solos, regarding my plays as
musical performances precisely as Shakespear did. As a
producer I went back to the forgotten heroic stage business and the exciting or impressive declamation I had
learnt from old-timers like Ristori, Salvini, and Barry
Sullivan. Yet so novel was my post-Marx post-Ibsen
outlook on life that nobody suspected that my methods
were as old as the stage itself.[26]

In this passage, written in 1933, Shaw could generalize
about what he doubtless was not consciously aware of
while he was writing his earlier plays; he could be a historian of a drama which he helped to create and observe his own role of reaction against Robertsonian
realism, Cup and Saucer respectability, and women
with pasts, both the women and the pasts usually well
constructed. Naturally, Shaw was piqued when he
read, in the 1940's, a description of his own plays as
well-made plays in the tradition of Scribe, and he attempted to prove to Allardyce Nicoll the inaccuracy of

97

his description. Indeed, he says, Nicoll's book made him jump, for, after all, was he not in the very act of rebellion against the school of Pinero, Grundy, and Sardou? What ingratitude for Professor Nicoll to lump him with the enemy![27] But Stephen Stanton and Martin Meisel have done the same,[28] intending to show that Shaw, for all his denunciation of the well-made play, was able to benefit from its techniques as Ibsen had done. But it is pretty clear, after all, that Shaw's plays, however well made, have as their substance an intellectual germ which is entirely lacking in the Scribean product. Would it not be more accurate to say that Shaw applied many of the principles of the well-made play to the establishment of an intellectual drama? For in the final analysis, what Shaw has in common with Scribe is not what has made Shaw's greatness. It was his distinctive genius alone that enabled him to be his own messiah.

Chapter 4

SHAKESPEARE AND ELIZABETHAN DRAMA

1. *Moral Defects of Shakespearean Drama*[1]

LIKE MOST of his comments on works of art, Shaw's dicta on Shakespeare are free from triviality and pedantic estheticism, for his judgments of life and literature were almost always in terms of his monolithic morality, a morality aerated with the vapors of German Idealism and existing beyond "good and evil." When Shakespeare is evaluated in such terms, the results are bound to be unconventional, surprising, and perhaps a bit irritating. But they are also enlightening because they make such little use of the inherited criteria of judgment and the inherited responses.

To begin with, Shaw disliked the Elizabethan sensibility, for to him it was like a rank plant in which the principle of life had become entirely unrestrained and wild while the impulses to organization and order had been repressed. One might say that the Elizabethans were entirely overcome by the irrational and chaotic Schopenhauerian Will to Live as opposed to Shaw's modification of it, the purposive Life Force. Shaw speaks with contempt of "the orgie [sic] called the Renaissance" (I, 130), and nominates the Elizabethan

99

as "the most despicable of all the ages in our history" (III, 298). And the chief instigator of the horrors of the age as they appear in literature was Christopher Marlowe:

Marlowe, the moment the exhaustion of the imaginative fit deprives him of the power of raving, becomes childish in thought, vulgar and wooden in humor, and stupid in his attempts at invention. He is the true Elizabethan blank-verse beast, itching to frighten other people with the superstitious terrors and cruelties in which he does not himself believe. . . . It is not surprising to learn that Marlowe was stabbed in a tavern brawl: what would be utterly unbelievable would be his having succeeded in stabbing anyone else. On paper the whole obscene crew of these blank-verse rhetoricians could outdare Lucifer himself: Nature can produce no murderer cruel enough for Webster, nor any hero bully enough for Chapman, devout disciples, both of them, of Kit Marlowe. But you do not believe in their martial ardor as you believe in the valor of Sidney or Cervantes. One calls the Elizabethan dramatists imaginative, as one might say the same of a man in delirium tremens. (II, 182)

There in brief is not only the trouble with the Elizabethans but the trouble with Shakespeare himself: lack of integrity, lack of belief, and lack of the courage of one's convictions (to have which one must first have convictions). Shaw, of course, is able to see the virtues of these dramatists, and most of all the virtues of Shakespeare. He is impressed by the beauty of much of their verse, though he admits that beautiful lines from Tourneur are like diamonds on a dungheap. He confesses that he could not avoid laughing at some of the low comedy, that Greene was amusing, that Jonson, though brutish, could produce pretty verses, that Beaumont and Fletcher, though humbugs (for Shaw a humbug is someone who assumes moral poses and has no morality of his own), could produce plays no worse than *The Lady of Lyons* (II, 183), but despite all of these small virtues the grave defects remain—"plays that have no ray of noble feeling, no touch of faith, beauty, or even common kindness in them from beginning to end" (I, 131).

That they are read at all, Shaw observes, is merely the result of reflected light from Shakespeare, who himself was dragged down by them and "since there was no other shop than theirs to serve his apprenticeship in, he had perforce to become an Elizabethan too" (III, 318). But for Shaw the Elizabethan dramatists have at least one very useful role—their existence can make it possible for us to purify Shakespeare's reputation from its spurious elements, to "cure people of admiring, as distinctly characteristic of Shakespear, the false, forced rhetoric, the callous sensation-mongering in murder and lust" (II, 183) from which undiscriminating bardolators obtain the same raptures which they obtain from the great elements of Shakespearean drama.

The key to Shaw's estimation of Shakespeare, as to so much else which interested him enough to write about it, is his puritanism. Puritanism, as the term may be applied to Shaw, although it embraces an attitude towards sex, has really no more to do with sex than anything else. A return to the original denotation of the word illuminates the matter: something is pure when it is unmixed. Puritanism is the law of identity in moral-imperative terms: a thing must *be* what it *claims* to be. The being and the claiming immediately suggest a conflict between the body and the mind, though the Schopenhauerian term is better: the Will to Live, rather than the body. This kind of puritanism, this insistence on integrity (again, in its original denotative sense of "wholeness" and "oneness"), this hatred of hypocrisy—this is the animating idea of virtually all of Shaw's works. Perhaps the idea is nowhere so clear as in the climax of *The Devil's Disciple*. Shaw, in a belated preface ("Three Plays for Puritans"), relates that even his early critics were unable to understand the moral conflict which Dick Dudgeon resolves in offering his life in place of Anderson's. Dick is a puritan because he believes that actions must be performed for their own intrinsic values, as gauged by intuition, and not for the sake of the values imposed upon the individual by society. And the most intrinsical act possible for Shaw is to be true to one's own nature. Since, according to the Schopenhauerian view, people will always do what they want anyway (although they may not know that they want to do it), the best thing, says Shaw, is to do it directly, purely and unmixedly. But most people, since they partake of a larger share of human weakness than the Shavian heroes, find that they must veil their personal inclinations (which come upon them they know not how) in pious trappings— in Freudian terms: defense mechanisms—supplied and approved by society as a whole. Thus, Mrs. Dudgeon, a sadist at heart, can be as much a sadist as she pleases by enacting her wickedness in the forms of publicly approved piety. As a result, she is the most "pious" yet the most immoral person in the play. Since everyone will follow his own will ultimately, the only morality for Shaw is to follow it openly and honestly, without pretending to be other than one is. If our basic human natures are given, are not the result of choice, are merely the Will to Live (cf. Freud's "id") as objecti-fied on the level of specific entities, honesty is the only morality. The irony of all this is that in Shaw's plays the heroes—that is, the people who are regarded as vil-lains by the "respectable" characters—are good, really Christianized people, to begin with.

The application of all of this to Shakespeare is quite simple: Shakespeare, says Shaw, did not have any strong, clear, profound opinions about man and the universe; he merely assumed in their stead an as-sortment of respectable platitudes which meant little to him. Thus, Shakespeare, our "immortal William," as Shaw calls him, was just another pious hypocrite with an adventitious morality. He lacked intellectual and artistic honesty. Painted in these colors, he be-comes the Keats of the Renaissance (as Keats tried to become the Shakespeare of the Romantics) who had a passion to drown himself in poesy but who had noth-ing to say. Shaw's criticism threw his contemporaries into outraged befuddlement, since Shakespeare was venerated like the Bible. But if the extremes charac-teristic of a revolutionary view are taken with a grain of salt, there is much in Shaw's approach which con-tributes new sensibility to the history of Shakespeare criticism.

One of Shaw's most powerful utterances about Shakespeare occurs in a review not of Shakespeare but of The Pilgrim's Progress dramatized for the stage:

. . . with extraordinary artistic powers, he understood nothing and believed nothing. Thirty-six big plays in five blank-verse acts, and (as Mr Ruskin, I think, once pointed out) not a single hero! Only one man in them all who believes in life, enjoys life, thinks life worth living, and has a sincere, unrhetorical tear dropped over his death-bed; and that man—Falstaff! What a crew they are—these Saturday to Monday athletic stockbroker Orlandos, these villains, fools, clowns, drunkards, cowards, intriguers, fighters, lovers, patriots, hypochondriacs who mistake themselves (and are mistaken by the author) for philosophers, princes without any sense of public duty, futile pessimists who imagine they are confronting a barren and unmeaning world when they are only contemplating their own worthlessness, self-seekers of all kinds, keenly observed and masterfully drawn from the romantic-commercial point of view. (III, 1-2)

The Shavian portraits of Shakespeare are portraits of a romantic poet par excellence, with plenty of invention but little brains. Shakespeare was the king of dramatists, as far as poetical faculties go, but in weighty matters of sociology and ethics he was a Simon Tappertit (III, 299). Most of Shakespeare's so-called profundities were to Shaw collections of "shallow proverbs in blank verse" (III, 344) "as exemplified in the remark that good and evil are mingled in our natures" (III, 200). Since most of Shakespeare's philosophic observations were platitudes of the age, Shaw finds Shakespeare unable to develop them. Instead, after introducing an idea that has the flavor of profundity, Shakespeare wanders off to other ideas that have the flavor of profundity. "The divinity which shapes our ends, rough hew them how we will, is mentioned fatalistically only to be forgotten immediately like a passing vague apprehension" (Prefaces, p. 630).

Shakespeare's great dramatic talent enabled him to produce realistic characters whom, too often, he was unable to put into realistic situations. But since this is characteristic of Elizabethan drama as a whole and, indeed, most drama before the time of Ibsen (by "realistic" Shaw means "experienced by the generality of mankind," a phrase which precludes experiences like incest and regicide), it is not so grave an objection as that which Shaw makes against the motivation of Shakespeare's characters. The motivation is external. Shaw's favorite illustration is *Othello*. Here is a play that is utterly melodramatic, that has not "a touch of character . . . below the skin" (III, 147). The jealousy is mere stage jealousy (as opposed to that of *The Winter's Tale*, Shaw notes). Iago is a trumpery character who makes stage effects and talks like Hamlet whenever possible. But what is particularly infuriating to Shaw is that students of the drama tend to see imaginary depths and "problems" in people like Iago and waste much time observing imaginary complexities of a character who has no character at all. So much in *Othello* is accidental and so much is the result of dramatic situations rather than the innermost nature of the figures of the play that Shakespeare, in this respect, *is* a precursor of Beaumont and Fletcher. For Shaw, all that *Othello* can offer as art is—and it is a good deal —passionate poetry. "Sense is drowned in sound. . . . Tested by the brain, it is ridiculous: tested by the ear, it is sublime" (III, 147-48). *Othello*, then, thrills us with poetic artistry, but "the moment a man has acquired sufficient reflective power to cease gaping at waxworks, he is on his way to losing interest in Othello, Desdemona, and Iago" (*Essays*, p. 141).[2] A certain countenance is given to Shaw's views here if we recall that the approach of A. C. Bradley was a fashionable one from the time of Coleridge to the beginning of the twentieth century. Bradley's analyses of the psyches of Shakespeare's tragic heroes are usually quite preposterous and refer more to imaginary real-life people than to characters in a play, who, after all, have no psyche available for analysis. There is no character underneath the words which present Hamlet, Othello, and the rest.

Shaw particularly liked to make fun of the bits of wisdom to be found in *Hamlet* and *As You Like It* and to contrast them with the wisdom of a modern like Ibsen. The greatest praise he can bestow is that they are "platitudinous fudge" by which no one but a village schoolmaster could be taken in (III, 344). The review of December 5, 1896, has an incisive discussion of Shakespeare's moral clichés. After quoting some lines from the speech in *As You Like It* containing: "If ever you have looked on better days,/ If ever been where bells have knolled to church," Shaw writes: "I really shall get sick if I quote any more of it. Was ever such canting, snivelling, hypocritical unctuousness exuded by an actor anxious to shew that he was above his profession, and was a thoroughly respectable man in private life? Why cannot all this putrescence be cut out of the play, and only the vital parts—the genuine story-telling, the fun, the poetry, the drama, be retained? Simply because, if nothing were left of Shakespear but his genius, our Shakespearolaters would miss all that they admire in him" (II, 269). But what is really revolting is that this platitudinous fudge is the very material out of which Hamlet and Prospero produce their observations:

> " 'And so, from hour to hour, we ripe and ripe;
> And then, from hour to hour, we rot and rot;
> And thereby hangs a tale.'

"Now considering that this fool's platitude is precisely the 'philosophy' of Hamlet, Macbeth ('Tomor-

row and tomorrow and tomorrow,' etc.), Prospero, and
the rest of them, there is something unendurably ag-
gravating in Shakespear giving himself airs with Touch-
stone, as if he, the immortal, ever, even at his sublimest,
had anything different or better to say himself (II,
267)."

When one considers the sophisticated morality of
The Devil's Disciple, the morality of the gratuitous act,
of goodness without sanction, one has no difficulty
understanding with what impatience Shaw viewed the
homely-homily morality of *As You Like It*. The review
of *As You Like It* concludes: "The production at this
Christmas season could not be more timely. The children will find the virtue of Adam and the philosophy
of Jaques just the thing for them; whilst their elders
will be delighted by the pageantry and the wrestling"
(II, 271).

For all his artistry, Shakespeare's trouble, as Shaw
puts it, is his lack of religion. He could mimic human
traits, he could create realistic characters from blood-
and-thunder source materials (although, as in the case
of Macbeth, there is often a clash between the relative
refinement of Shakespeare's own nature and the coarse-
ness of the original character), and he could take ref-
uge from despair by making jokes out of the cruelties
of nature and calling us the gods' tennis-balls, "but
with all his gifts, the fact remains that he never found
the inspiration to write an original play" (*Prefaces*, p.
543). When Shaw speaks of an "original" play, he
means a work which presents a genuine view or *aperçu*
of human life. It is true that to many readers Shakespeare, in seeming to be a pessimist, seems to have a
view of human life. Hamlet is made to wander onstage
and make observations about the human condition

which are bleak fruits of depression. But this amounts to "agonizing in a void," because such observations are not the result of any coherent philosophy. They are the attitudinizings of a poseur: ". . . a novice can read his plays from one end to the other without learning that the world is finally governed by forces expressing themselves in religions and laws which make epochs rather than by vulgarly ambitious individuals who make rows" (*Prefaces*, p. 630). Although pessimism is a respectable attitude, there is, says Shaw, intellectually honest and intellectually dishonest pessimism. What makes Shakespeare's despair dishonest is that it is usually voiced by characters who are disappointed with the universe because it has not served them up a happy life on a silver spoon. The Shakspearean pessimists, like Timon, for example, paint for themselves what is a rhetorical and unreal picture of human nature to begin with and then lash out at the world of men for not living up to it. This is like a man who accidentally drinks poison and then blames the poison for not being honey. The poison never pretended to be honey. But Shaw finds that not only does Shakespeare allow his characters to have a dark view of a world whose darkness they themselves have created, he refuses to face the dark view honestly and squarely, avoiding all consequences of such a view by introducing "flights of angels." This is the artistic equivalent of an atheist saying prayers on the death of his friend simply because he has no idea what else to do. It reflects weakness of character, Shaw might say, to see a meaningless or hostile world and then to evade the consequences of such a view by invoking a traditional formula which is just another element of the same meaningless world. For Shaw, the shortcomings which Shakespeare saw in men were due not to men but to Shakespeare's ignorance of what men were and what the world was and what the role of men was in the world.

Chesterton finds Shaw's denunciation of Shakespeare's pessimism to be the result of misunderstanding: "Shaw, I think, has entirely misunderstood the pessimistic passages of Shakespeare. They are flying moods which a man with a fixed faith can afford to entertain. That all is vanity, that life is dust and love is ashes, these are frivolities, these are jokes that a Catholic can afford to utter."[3] It is amusing to note that Frank Harris accounted for Shakespeare's pessimism as the result of having had his heart broken by the dark lady of the sonnets, an absurd notion, which Shaw rejects with the characteristisic comment that Shakespeare was too ironic and satiric to allow his whole sensibility to be infected by something so trivial as romantic passion (*Prefaces*, p. 764).

What, one might ask, is the basis for Shaw's criticism of Shakespeare's lack of religion? Religion is, of course, a loaded word by which Shaw means a pattern or idea according to which man may form himself. As a believer in creative evolution and as a reader familiar with a fair share of nineteenth-century German philosophy, Shaw believed that man could influence his own biological future and that he could create the reality of his own nature, since that nature was essentially psychological. If reality is psychological and not "given," then pessimism *is* barren because man can be whatever he wants to be. The problem that remains, however, is: how do you make men want to be their best selves? Probably through the arts in general and Shavian drama in particular, although Shaw was rather reluctant to admit that people were really educable.

Ideally, breeding new people through the practice of eugenics is his plan. In practice, however, Shaw believed in the power of the arts to refine the nature of man, provided that a given man had normal faculties. How bizarre of him to have preached on the platform and in his plays and prose if he did not believe any good could come of them! In addition, education for Shaw did not mean instilling qualities that had no existence at all in the student, but, rather, teaching the student to exploit, for self-development, his already given personality. Elimination of the sense of sin (i.e., acceptance of one's id) is a typical Shavian platform for education. But whatever the answer, the rejection of the world on the grounds that it is unalterably what it is and that we are an unalterable part of it, is irresponsible.

Curiously enough, for Shaw the prime instance of a religion of hope and aspiration was *The Pilgrim's Progress.* For, as one writer has explained it, Bunyan is preferable to Shakespeare "because he saw the virtue of identifying oneself with 'the purpose of the world as he understood it,' whereas the author of tragedies sees only the frequent defeat of trivial personal aims."[4]

All that you miss in Shakespear you find in Bunyan, to whom the true heroic came quite obviously and naturally. The world was to him a more terrible place than it was to Shakespear; but he saw through it a path at the end of which a man might look not only forward to the Celestial City but back on his life and say:— "Tho' with great difficulty I am got hither, yet now I do not repent me of all the trouble I have been at to arrive where I am. My sword I give to him that shall succeed me in my pilgrimage, and my courage and skill to him that can get them." The heart vibrates like a bell to such an utterance as this: to turn from it to "Out, out, brief candle," and "The rest is silence," and "We are such stuff as dreams are made of; and our little life is rounded by a sleep" is to turn from life, strength, resolution, morning air and eternal youth, to the terrors of a drunken nightmare. (III, 2)

Whereas Bunyan writes from conviction, Shakespeare is unable to write without betraying "the paper origin of his fancies" (III, 3). Shaw makes fun of Shakespeare's literary allusions and wishes that his "little Latin" had been less, "like his Greek!" At least, however, Shaw admits that Shakespeare emerged from his literary vices not as a Bohemian but as a snob: he raised a cynical outlook to "something like sublimity in his tragedies" and dramatized "morbid, self-centred passions and . . . feeble and shallow speculations," exhibiting wit and poetry in the process (III, 4).

Now that Shaw's specific objections to Shakespeare have been shown (and a few of his redeeming virtues), who are the artists in comparison to whom Shakespeare falls short? The answer is simple: Goethe, Wagner, and Ibsen. Can people bred on Goethe, Wagner, and Ibsen be expected, asks Shaw, to endure the twaddle of the Seven Ages of Man or Hamlet on suicide?

This brings us to the question of the role which evolution plays in the arts. For what is the advantage which Goethe, Wagner, and Ibsen have over Shakespeare? Mainly that they are modern. Besides the obvious advantages of contemporaneity, what other benefits does the fact that they are modern confer? This most important benefit, surely: that their minds and the minds of their audience are able to entertain matters of greater complexity, subtlety, and sophistication than the minds of Shakespeare and his audience. This is not owing to any physical evolution of the mind during the past few hundred years but mainly to the availability to both artist and audience of several hundred more years of civilization. This is an inestimable advantage, for more years of intellectual and esthetic heritage mean that more thoughts and feelings and degrees of feelings are also available. Thus, works of art of greater organization and complexity and audiences able to appreciate them are possible. For there to be a Henry James, a Jane Austen and a Meredith must have gone before. And the Henry James will be the more exquisite, the range of play of his feelings and his equipment for conveying them will be the more varied and subtle than those of his artist-forebears. Furthermore, his art will be able to deal with the increased depth and complexity of the age and society in which he creates. Thus, we have a great increase in esthetic materials. And Shaw's argument is that the mind which has been taxed and exploited by an Ibsen will find itself incompletely taxed by a Shakespeare. "There is no eminent writer, not even Sir Walter Scott, whom I can despise so entirely as I despise Shakespear when I measure my mind against his" (II, 195).

For the range and delicacy of the mind of a Shaw *is*, if for no other reason than its access to three more centuries of civilization, superior to the range and delicacy of Shakespeare's mind. Shaw himself is the first to admit that his own superiority is not in technical skill, for in poetry Shakespeare is still a nonpareil, but in the developed mind provided by additional civilization. In Shakespearean verse no one has ever surpassed or even equaled Shakespeare. But, claims Shaw, in thought, in profundity and complexity, how far behind must Shakespeare remain! Just as, some day, we ourselves will seem primitive to future moderns—but not in artistry. Is not this view of art once again a fruit of the Hegelian synthetic view of civilization? And it is a kind of view consistent with Shaw's general outlook, which is Platonic, Hegelian, and which ends, in *Back to Methuselah*, with that unheard, non-sensuous, ideal music so indigenous to an idealist philosophy. One need only consider the emotions one feels in listening to a Gregorian chant and compare them with the emotions one feels in listening to *Tristan*, for instance. In its way, the chant is an absolute experience offering its own peculiar emotion. There can be no "improvement" on it. On the other hand, the faculties which have experienced and grasped *Tristan* will feel not fully taxed by a steady diet of chants, no matter how esthetically pleasing the chants may be. And in the arts, besides this esthetic enlargement, there is an intellectual enlargement. Shaw described this with great lucidity in connection with Clement Scott's inability to appreciate Ibsen:

Like all energetic spirits, he was a pioneer at first, fighting for the return to nature in Robertson's plays against the stagey stuff which he found in possession of the theatre. Since that time the unresting march of evolution has brought us past Robertson. Our feeling has developed and put new thoughts into our heads; and our brains have developed and interpreted our feelings to us more critically. Ideas which were formerly only conceived by men of genius like Ibsen, or intensely energetic spirits like Nietzsche, are freely used by dramatists like Sudermann, and are beginning to creep into quite ordinary plays, just as I can remember the pet discords of Schumann and Wagner beginning to creep into the music-hall after a period of fashionable novelty in the drawing room. (II, 142)

Shaw's irritation at idolatry of Shakespeare, then, is irritation at that ignorance which supposes that because Shakespeare's poetry is great poetry his thought must also be great thought. But, he says, not only are his thoughts obsolete—they were never profound in the first place. Surely, Shaw insists, no educated person today can have much serious interest in Shakespeare's social views, except as historical curiosa. "Even when Shakespear, in his efforts to be a social philosopher, does rise for an instant to the level of a sixth-rate Kingsley, his solemn self-complacency infuriates me. And yet, so wonderful is his art, that it is not easy to disentangle what is unbearable from what is irresistible" (II, 268). Here we see the distinction which Shaw makes between the art and its content. The rumpus which Shaw caused by inquiring whether in one sense he was not better than Shakespeare is seen to be the result of his not being understood by the bardolaters who thought he was challenging Shakespeare's genius.

As Shakespear in drama, like Mozart in opera, and Michael Angelo in fresco, reached the summit of his art, nobody can be better than Shakespear, though anybody may now have things to say that Shakespear did not say, and outlooks on life and character which were not open to him. (*Self-Sketches*, p. 190)

It was the overwhelming contrast with Ibsen that explains my Saturday Review campaign against the spurious part of Shakespear's reputation. But the notion that I ever claimed crudely that my plays, or anybody's plays, were better written than Shakespear's is absurd. (*Self-Sketches*, pp. 153-54)

Since Shaw regarded Ibsen as primarily a social reformer (which Ibsen himself said he was not) who
spoke for the age, what chance could Shakespeare have
in competition with such a man as Ibsen? Creative
evolution works in the arts as in life—there is a succession of artists each more conscious and aware than
those who came before. No one is final and everyone
will be synthesized into the next great creator. If this
is the case, Shakespeare, explains one of Shaw's critics,
"must be seen in relation to the long story of the slow
evolution of the mind and character of man. Looked
upon so, he diminishes, Shaw argued: often his laughter is coarse; his characters hollow; his themes trite; his
treatment of sex sensual, romantic, and immoral; his
politics execrable."[5]

When we examine the criteria wherewith Shaw re-
moves Shakespeare, or at least one leg of Shakespeare,
from his pedestal, we see that they imply a functional
and didactic view of art. For not only did Shakespeare
fail to give insight into eternal problems, he failed to
manifest a serious interest in the social problems of his
age, whereas Ibsen thought freshly about eternal and
local problems. Insofar as Shakespeare did make an
eternal contribution, it was the contribution of great
poetry. But in literature, beauty was not enough for
Shaw. One had to be a Shelley, an Ibsen, a Morris.
This indicates no deficiency in Shaw's esthetic faculties, which were exquisitely developed; for Shaw's love
of and understanding of music are the mark of anything but a bogus esthete. But when meaning is added
to beauty of sound, Shaw's puritanism (as I have explained puritanism above) demanded that the result
be more than, as he put it, sublime balderdash. To
Shaw, language implies the obligation of good sense,

and literature the obligation of contributing insights into man and society. On the other hand, Shaw's poetic faculties were not a particular strength. While he was maximally equipped to appreciate music, other types of what Susanne Langer calls "presentational forms" were not readily accessible to him. He could appreciate non-verbal forms, but once words were used, he expected considerable intellectual lucidity from them. In fairness to Shaw, however, one must point out that in his plays he achieved a subtlety of effect from language that he could not always appreciate in other writers.

The plays of Shakespeare which Shaw liked best were the problem plays and *Hamlet.* For those dark comedies were more realistic to him in their lack of romantic sentiment about life, and in what to him was an anticipation of Ibsen, than *Othello* and *Romeo.* *Othello,* to a practiced eye of the theater like Shaw's, had all the stage types of popular melodrama: "Its noble savage, its villain, its funny man, its carefully assorted pathetic and heavy feminine interest, its smothering and suicide, its police-court morality and commonplace thought" (III, 315). There is constant praise of *All's Well's* defiance of stagey devices and stagey characters (see III, 2; III, 245), and what could be more true to the Shavian view of life than the heroine chasing the young man and regarding the business of marriage with grim seriousness? "The ordinary lover of Shakespear would . . . demur to my placing his popular catchpenny plays, of which As You Like It is an avowed type, below true Shakespearean plays like Measure for Measure. I cannot help that. Popular dramas and operas may have overwhelming merits as enchanting make-believes; but a poet's sincerest vision of the world must always take precedence of his prettiest fool's paradise" (*Essays*, p. 164).

Hamlet is the one major Shakespearean character whom Shaw exalts, for in him "the common personal passions are so superseded by wider and rarer interests, and so discouraged by a degree of critical self-consciousness which makes the practical efficiency of the instinctive man on the lower plane impossible to him, that he finds the duties dictated by conventional revenge and ambition as disagreeable a burden as commerce is to a poet. Even his instinctive sexual impulses offend his intellect; so that when he meets the woman who excites them he invites her to join him in a bitter and scornful criticism of their joint absurdity" (III, 201-02). Instead of the usual compliance with conventional sentiment and conventional morality, Hamlet exhibits ethical questioning, a "revolt of his feelings against ready-made morality" (*Prefaces*, p. 688). Hamlet is a Renaissance John Tanner who experiences conflict between convention and will, and like Dick Dudgeon Hamlet cannot determine the correct course of behavior by referring to the accepted ethical code. Instead, he conforms to the incognizable he-knows-not-what of his own essential self. In *Hamlet* Shakespeare transcends his blood-and-thunder source materials and becomes a higher agent of the Life Force.[6] And most important, in *Hamlet* we see a rare operation of Shakespeare's religious sense:

Here, too, Shakespear betrays for once his religious sense by making Hamlet, in his agony of shame, declare that his mother's conduct makes "sweet religion a rhapsody of words." But for that passage we might almost suppose that the feeling of Sunday morning in the country which Orlando describes so perfectly in As

You Like It was the beginning and end of Shakespear's notion of religion. I say almost, because Isabella in Measure for Measure has religious charm, in spite of the conventional theatrical assumption that female religion means an inhumanly ferocious chastity. But for the most part Shakespear differentiates his heroes from his villains much more by what they do than by what they are. (*Prefaces*, p. 761)

In sum, Shaw's criticisms of Shakespeare come down to this: he lacked moral conviction, he was not interested in the social problems of his time, he had a delicate sensibility but could rarely create a perfect fusion of his crude sources with his own nature. What do these criticisms indicate about Shaw himself? Most strikingly that he disliked both tragedy and romance (which we can see by observing his own plays), for, to his way of thinking, tragedy and romance are ultimately irresponsible and unrealistic views of human life. As he remarks in connection with Ibsen, the tragedy is that there is no tragedy, that life goes on, that smotherings and suicides and poisons do not put an end to human problems in normal life. As for romance, romance pretends that people are other than they are, more beautiful, more good, more unselfish. Both views, the tragic and the romantic, make the fatal assumption that there are villains and heroes. It is in this more than in anything else that Shaw's own plays differ from those of Shakespeare. For him, then, there is no ground for a thoroughgoing pessimism, for human nature is not all bad, and since creative evolution is always in action, the better elements are engaged in a moral equivalent of the survival of the fittest. As for the idealization of love, which is the stock-in-trade of romance, this is the complement of pessimism, assuming that people are more than human in their physical and moral constitutions. Sen Gupta, in his book on Shaw, is perhaps too hard on Shaw when he remarks: "The defect of Shaw's criticism of Shakespeare is that Shaw has an inherent inability to understand literature that is romantic and poetical. With Ibsen, he treads on much safer ground, because Ibsen's dramas are largely a war on the ideals of Capitalistic civilization."[7] It was not an "inability to understand" tragedy and poetry, but a puritanical objection to the poetic emphases of tragedy and romance, emphases of the sort he denounces at great length in his discussions of the wickedness of ideals in *The Quintessence of Ibsenism*. The sensuous attractions of the poetical experience were vitiated for him by the fact that poetical constructions have referents which he could not accept, whereas musical constructions do not have referents.

2. *Shakespeare's Word Music*

For Shaw his "word music" above all entitled Shakespeare to eminence. Unfortunately, when Shaw speaks of "word music" he does so with the assumption that sound is quite detachable from sense and that, since Shakespeare's thought is puerile but his verse pleasing, the beauty of the verse must be in the sound. A few examples will illustrate:

. . . only a musician can understand the play of feeling which is the real rarity in his early plays. . . . the score and not the libretto . . . keeps the work alive and fresh. (I, 24)
Shakespear shews himself in it a commonplace librettist working on a stolen plot, but a great musician. (III, 322)
For the most part, one has to listen to the music of Shakespear—in which music, I repeat . . . the whole

worth and charm of these early plays of his lies. (I, 204)

. . . comparatively few of Shakespear's admirers are at all conscious that they are listening to music as they hear his phrases turn and his lines fall so fascinatingly and memorably. (III, 323)

Finally, he writes to Mrs. Campbell: "When you play Shakespear, dont worry about the character, but go for the music. It was by word music that he expressed what he wanted to express; and if you get the music right, the whole thing will come right."[8] Furthermore, Shaw has said in a number of his reviews of Shakespeare that if you were to paraphrase some of his most famous speeches you would see at once that all their greatness lies not in the meaning, which is quite commonplace, but in the word music.

One does not have to go quite so far as to share Cleanth Brooks' horror of the "heresy of paraphrase" to see that there is something fundamentally unsound and not entirely clear about Shaw's insistence on Shakespearean word music. For the supposed beauty of the sound is most tightly bound up with the meaning of the words. If there is any beauty in calling a life a "brief candle" it is more than "word music" which produces this beauty, for is "brief candle" sonically more beautiful than "breece cannel"? Surely the idea of life as a candle must contribute a good deal to the total effect. No matter how shallow and platitudinous Shakespeare's thoughts may be, the beautiful "word music" is hardly unrelated to the liberties of poetic language.

One feels, when reading a passage like the following, that Shaw does not quite know what he is talking about: "Shakespear is so much the word musician

that mere practical intelligence . . . cannot enable anybody to understand his works or arrive at a right execution of them without the guidance of a fine ear."
For the sound redeems "the poverty of meaning. In
fact, we have got so far beyond Shakespear as a man of
ideas that there is by this time hardly a famous passage
in his works that is considered fine on any other ground
than that it sounds beautifully. . . . Strip it of that
beauty of sound by prosaic paraphrase, and you have
nothing left but a platitude" (III, 76). One is accustomed to better sense from Shaw than this, for strip
any poetry of sound by paraphrasing it and of course
what is left is undistinguished. Poetry is not philosophy, but it is poetry. Can one take away the poetry and
expect the residue to be philosophy?

At least Shaw was on safer esthetic ground when
he used his reviews to encourage players of Shakespeare to pay more heed to their diction. Of a performance of *Julius Caesar* in 1898 Shaw wrote: "What is
missing in the performance, for want of the specific
Shakespearean skill, is the Shakespearean music" (III,
301). Again, in a review of *Much Ado*, a play which
Shaw disliked, he complained that the actors do not
pay attention to the words: "Nothing but the music
of the words—above all, not their meaning—can save
the part" (III, 325). He constantly speaks in terms of
opera and directs the actors to attend to the "tongue's
sweet air" even if they do not understand what they
are saying (I, 25). For the most part, audiences are
not interested in the beauty of verse and want stage
business and excitement. When Shaw praised Kate
Rourke for her musical performance of Helena in *A
Midsummer Night's Dream*, she was embarrassed and

admitted that that performance had been considered a failure.[9]

For all his objections to Shakespeare, Shaw probably did more to encourage authentic Elizabethan performance of Shakespeare's plays than people who professed to love him more. In a review of *Antony and Cleopatra* in 1897, Shaw speaks against one of the modern practices that ruin Shakespeare's verse—the practice of pronouncing it like prose in order to avoid "singsong." After quoting the "Oh withered is the garland of the war" speech from *Antony*, Shaw writes:

This is not good sense—not even good grammar. If you ask what does it all mean, the reply must be that it means just what its utterer feels. The chaos of its thought is a reflection of her mind, in which one can vaguely discern a wild illusion that all human distinction perishes with the gigantic distinction between Antony and the rest of the world. Now it is only in music, verbal or other, that the feeling which plunges thought into confusion can be artistically expressed. Any attempt to deliver such music prosaically would be as absurd as an attempt to speak an oratorio of Handel's, repetitions and all. The right way to declaim Shakespear is the sing-song way. Mere metric accuracy is nothing. There must be beauty of tone, expressive inflection, and infinite variety of *nuance* to sustain the fascination of the infinite monotony of the chanting. (III, 77)

I cannot explain what "the infinite monotony of the chanting" means, but the passage is otherwise in harmony with enlightened modern views of Shakespearean performance, if not with the current practice. Shaw had a good deal to say about modern treatments and desecrations of Shakespeare, almost all of which applies as well today as in the nineties. If the Granville Barker performances in the early part of this century were a step forward, our modern television performances, directed towards the prosaic minds of philistine masses, are a step backward which makes Shaw's insights especially timely.

3. *Shakespeare in the Nineties*

The performances of Shakespeare's plays in Shaw's time were in many respects like the performances in our own. They employed the titles of the Shakespearean original and a good many of the lines, but the chief attractions were scenery, music, slapstick, and fancy acting. Little wonder that Shaw found them boring, for as spectacle they were tied to an original which hampered them, and as Shakespeare they were relatively unintelligible, for besides the cuts and alterations to spoil them, there was the poor diction, usually hasty, of the actors.

When the staging was fancy, Shaw protested that every new accessory "is brought in at the deadliest risk of destroying the magic spell woven by the poet" (I, 179). The more lavish the production, the more fruitless the presentation of Shakespeare. The more money and ornament bestowed on the plays, the more boring they become. The only hope Shaw could voice was that every revival would help "to exhaust the number of possible ways of altering Shakespear's plays unsuccessfully" (I, 198). The scene painter, the costumier, the actor-manager—all these used Shakespeare as a vehicle for their talents, while Shakespeare was mutilated to the point of incoherence.

In an article which appeared in the *Stratford-upon-Avon Herald* in 1923, Shaw gave a brief summary of the downhill march of Shakespearean production in England.[10] He said that Shakespeare had really been exiled from the stage for 250 years, while Garrick, Siddons, Irving, *et al.* pretended to be doing his plays. Audiences gradually came to be interested in scenery and spectacle, which is inappropriate to Shakespeare's plays. In addition, the uninterrupted procession of scenes, characteristic of Elizabethan drama, was replaced by five acts, framed in a proscenium, with frequent intermissions, which changed the flavor and character of the plays. By the time of Ellen Terry, the living tableau had taken the place of the fast-moving Elizabethan series of scenes. Along with this arose the custom of playing music during the performance. But the very worst practice, one which began shortly after Shakespeare's time and continued until the time of Granville Barker, was the excision from and alteration of the text. In a review of *The Two Gentlemen of Verona,* which he entitled "Poor Shakespear!" Shaw wrote:

The piece founded by Augustin Daly on Shakespear's Two Gentlemen of Verona, to which I looked forward last week, is not exactly a comic opera, though there is plenty of music in it, and not exactly a serpentine dance, though it proceeds under a play of changing colored lights. It is something more old-fashioned than either: to wit, a vaudeville. . . . In preparing the text of his version, Mr Daly has proceeded on the usual principles, altering, transposing, omitting, improving, correcting, and transferring speeches from one character to another. Many of Shakespear's lines are mere poetry, not to the point, not getting the play along, evidently stuck in because the poet liked to spread himself in verse. On all such unbusinesslike superfluities Mr Daly is down with his blue pencil. (I, 170-71)

The chief mutilators tend to be those people who admire Shakespeare the most (*Prefaces*, p. 750), such as Augustin Daly himself. But actors and actor-managers are not particularly scrupulous in their fidelity to the original texts. After seeing his production of *Hamlet*, Shaw wrote a letter to John Barrymore:

Shakespear, with all his shortcomings, was a very great playwright; and the actor who undertakes to improve his plays undertakes thereby to excel to an extraordinary degree in two professions in both of which the highest success is extremely rare. Shakespear himself, though by no means a modest man, did not pretend to be able to play Hamlet as well as write it; he was content to do a recitation in the dark as the ghost. But you have ventured not only to act Hamlet, but to discard about a third of Shakespear's script and substitute stuff of your own. . . . you say, in effect, "I am not going to read Hamlet at all: I am going to leave it out. But see what I give you in exchange!" . . . Hamlet—Shakespear's Hamlet—can be done from end to end in four hours . . . and it never flags nor bores. Done in any other way Shakespear is the worst of bores, because he has to be chopped into a mere cold stew. I prefer my way. I wish you would try it, and concentrate on acting rather than on authorship, at which, believe me, Shakespear can write your head off.[11]

In many of the Shakespeare reviews, Shaw claimed that people had been trying for years to convince the managers to do Shakespeare plays as written. To Shaw this meant doing them swiftly, but distinctly, by omitting the intermissions, the dumb shows, and the superfluous stage business. Over and over again Shaw reminds us of how plays were performed in Shakespeare's day, one scene rapidly following another. Modern intermissions are for the benefit of the scene shifters and the lemonade vendors and have nothing to do with Shakespeare. Once you let in the scene shifters and the lemonade vendors, a good deal of Shakespeare must be left out if you wish to have the performance take less than four hours. In the essay "The Religion of the Pianoforte," Shaw observes that he had seen eight performances of *Hamlet* by the year 1894 and had he not known the play well from his readings he would never have found out about the roles of such characters as Fortinbras, because they were always cut to save time.

Chief of the Shakespeare mutilators was Sir Henry Irving. Although the delicacy and introspective quality of his acting of Hamlet is attested to by Shaw himself, as well as other critics, like Max Beerbohm, there is also general agreement on Irving's limitations. In a review of Irving's *Cymbeline*, Shaw wrote that Irving "does not merely cut plays: he disembowels them. In Cymbeline he has quite surpassed himself by extirpating the antiphonal third verse of the famous dirge. A man who would do that would do anything" (II, 198). Irving's only rival in Shakespearean infamy was perhaps Beerbohm Tree, "for whom Shakespear does not exist at all." Tree, of generous nature, says Shaw, wrote plays of his own which he attributed to Shakespeare, manufacturing unlimited stage business and speaking blank verse unintelligibly.[12]

Throughout the drama reviews of the nineties the only praise which Shaw gives to performances of Shakespeare and Elizabethan drama is to the renderings of the Elizabethan Stage Society. A bit later he was able to add Forbes Robertson and Granville Barker to his list of intelligent executors of Elizabethan plays. "It is only within the last few years that some of our younger actor-managers have been struck with the idea, quite novel in their profession, of performing Shakespear's plays as he wrote them" (*Prefaces*, p. 723). Many years later, looking back at the radical performances of Granville Barker, Shaw wrote: "Mr. Harley Granville-Barker, developing certain experiments made from time to time by Mr William Poel, another Englishman, inaugurated twentieth century Shakespear by a series of performances in which the plays were given with unprecedented artistic splendor without the omission of a single decently presentable line, undivided into acts, without the old pictorial scenery, and with, as a result, a blessed revelation of Shakespear as the Prince of Entertainers instead of the most dreaded of bores, and a degree of illusion which the pictorial theatre had not only failed to attain, but had sedulously destroyed" (*Essays*, p. 155).

The reforms of the Elizabethan Stage Society were manifold: the speaking of the actors was slowed down so that the poetry became intelligible and absorbing, and since the star-system was not in effect (because the performers were not stars) the actors showed more interest in their lines than in themselves. The Society avoided scenery, leaving the audience's imagination free to picture the scenes suggested by the poetry. "The poetry of The Tempest is so magical that it would make the scenery of a modern theatre ridiculous" (III, 241). Shaw did not see how the addition of scenery to the Society's production of *The Tempest* could have improved it. Would that Sir Henry Irving felt the same way, he adds, for the imagination is so much more vivid than painted scenery that scenery detracts from the experience of the play, especially in *The Tempest* or *A Midsummer Night's Dream*; but in a play like *Othello* Shaw did not think scenery would be amiss (III, 215).[13] The Society used a stage which resembled the stage of Shakespeare's day, with a platform jutting out into the audience. Later in his life, Shaw praised the movies for their ability to do what Shakespeare's stage was able to do: bring the drama close to the audience. The proscenium of the nineteenth century was an impediment between performer and audience and encouraged the producer to arrange his performance into tableaux. When the Elizabethan Stage Society did *Twelfth Night* Shaw wrote:

The performance of Twelfth Night now in question brought out another point with remarkable distinctness, and that was the immense advantage of the platform stage to the actor. It places him in so intimate a relation to the spectators that the difficulty of getting delicate play "across the footlights," and of making vehement play forcible enough to overcome the remoteness of the "living picture" stage, all but vanishes. . . . I am convinced that if Burbage were to rise from the dead and accept an invitation from Sir Henry Irving to appear at the Lyceum, he would recoil beaten the moment he realized that he was to be looked at as part of an optical illusion through a huge hole in the wall, instead of being practically in the middle of the theatre. (I, 189-90)

Shaw's attitude toward Shakespeare was the product of two pervasive esthetic intentions. The first was to purify works of art from spurious accouterments which distort them and degrade their character. Whether it was the use of old instruments and small choruses for performing Handel and Bach or the elimination of elaborate scenery, extraneous action, and a tendency to speak blank verse as prose in performances of Shakespeare, the intent was to clarify the real nature and character of the esthetic object. Shaw's second intention was to emphasize what is contemporary and to encourage it. His concern with progress and Creative Evolution, while entirely appropriate in the realms of sociology, science, and morals, tended to insist that works of art display an ideology which could be swallowed by his contemporaries and nourish them sufficiently to turn them into predecessors, at least, of the superman. Shakespeare's ideas, stemming as they did from an aristocratic and privileged society, were peculiarly unsuited, in Shaw's view, for nourishing modern man. When he was not soapboxing—and especially when he had to deal with music—Shaw was perfectly able to see that a real chasm separated esthetics and ideology. But literature's dependence upon ideas made it difficult for him to purify his literary evaluations from a judgment of the current validity of the ideas themselves. As a result, he was apt to give too much weight to the presence or absence of "progressive" ideas in the literary works he had to consider. But as he got older—and further away in years from his campaigns of the nineties—his preoccupation with ideas in literary works tended to decrease. He came to speak more approvingly and on more purely esthetic grounds of works toward which he had been harsh in his younger days. Even with regard to Shakespeare we can see a change in his later pronouncements. In the famous "Better than Shakespear?" section of the preface to "Three Plays for Puritans," Shaw looked back on the controversy and wrote: "It was the age of gross ignorance of Shakespear and incapacity for his works that produced the indiscriminate eulogies with which we are familiar. It was the revival of serious attention to those works that coincided with the movement for giving genuine instead of spurious and silly representations of his plays. So much for Bardolatry!" (*Prefaces*, p. 750)

Chapter 5

IBSEN

IN CONTRAST to the drama which had gone before—the drama of romance, of polite society, of the well-made play, and of the police court—Ibsen was indeed the new drama. And it was his serious and fresh treatment of morality which spoke so directly to the mind of Shaw. Yet the general critical opinion of Shaw's championship of Ibsen is that Shaw admired Ibsen not so much for holding the mirror up to nature as holding the mirror up to Shaw. It has also been said more than once that *The Quintessence of Ibsenism* is really a book about Shaw himself. But to counterbalance these facts, the critics have also conceded that Shaw's treatment of Ibsen's plays of the middle period is fairly true to the plays themselves, perhaps with an exaggerated emphasis here and there. Happily enough, it is plays of the middle period which Shaw most frequently discusses and which people most frequently read, so that his less conventional appreciations of *Emperor and Galilean* and *Peer Gynt* need not be insisted upon.

Above all, Ibsen stood as the herald of the new drama and the serious spirit which came to be so much a part of Shaw's own life. And representing a new spirit, a spirit of rebellion and revolt, Ibsen became the modern Good Man of art in Shaw's private heaven and hell. For Shaw himself has said, with reference to Ibsen, that all progress involves the destruction of the old order. Indeed, there is an aphorism in "The Revolutionist's Handbook" which says as much. Just as many of Ibsen's characters (though not as many as Shaw would lead us to believe) rebel against the old morality, so Ibsen himself, in Shaw's eyes, was a rebel not only against the old morality but against the old art. In fact, Ibsen was, for Shaw, the literary counterpart of Wagner, rejecting old forms and old subjects. Naturally, the villains of Shaw's theatrical cosmos were the men who did nothing to further the cause of Ibsen or, even worse, who actively hindered it.

These men were no less than the majority of actors, managers, and critics of the nineties. In 1898, more than forty years after Ibsen had begun to write plays and more than eight years after William Archer began to write his translations, the status of Ibsen in England was such that Shaw could write:

The English theatre distinguished itself last week. The occasion was Ibsen's seventieth birthday. On the Continent it was celebrated by special representations of his works. The English theatre took not the smallest notice of Ibsen, but gave an enthusiastic and unprecedented benefit to Miss Nellie Farren. This is quite as it should be. It expresses the real condition of dramatic art in this country with just the characteristic British touch of caricature. Sir Henry Irving and the other leaders of his profession probably feel proud of it. Mr Beerbohm Tree, who ventured to contribute three guineas towards the purchase of a drinking cup for Ibsen (all Norwegians are assumed to be mighty drinkers), must feel rather like a man in morning dress at a smart dinner-party; for no other manager compromised himself by meddling in the business. And the managers were quite right. They are not in Ibsen's line; and Ibsen is not in theirs. He has seated himself over their heads without the slightest assistance from them, or the faintest comprehension on their part why or how he was establishing himself on high without their having voice or part in the matter. (III, 341-42)

Irving, Shaw had virtually given up as hopeless. Although it was surely Irving's duty, as leader of the theater of his day, to show interest in the Ibsen cause, he had not done so. For after all, as the exponent of the Self-Expounded, "How can he bring his transfigurations and fantasies to bear on the realities of the modern school?" (III, 31).

The managers on the whole were not interested in producing Ibsen, because his plays did not set them or their actors off very well. There was little opportunity for lavish stagings and for imaginative "interpretations," and the managers themselves were perhaps not quite intellectual enough to understand the plays (III, 28-29). And it was a matter of fact that the commercial managers were not responsible for the performances of Ibsen which did take place, scarce as they were. Edmund Gosse was principally responsible for writing about Ibsen and thereby making him a relatively familiar name, even before his plays were available in English.[1] From 1872-79 Gosse wrote nine articles on Ibsen and in 1879 published his *Studies in the Literature of Northern Europe.* The first London performance of an Ibsen play took place in December, 1880, when William Archer's adaptation of *Pillars of*

Society was given once at the Gaiety Theatre. Later, *Breaking a Butterfly*, an adaptation of *A Doll's House* by Henry Arthur Jones which gave the play a happy ending, was performed in 1884. (Many years afterwards, Jones apologized for his massacre of the play.) Then, in 1889, the famous performance of *A Doll's House* by Janet Achurch and Charles Charrington was given, about which Shaw had much to say. In 1891, J. T. Grein established the Independent Theatre and began its brief life with a production of *Ghosts*, and it was Elizabeth Robins who in 1896 was enabled to produce *Little Eyolf* on the fruits of a subscription. Shaw's only consolation was the belief, questionable perhaps, that although very little Ibsen was produced it was enough to begin to refine the taste of the audience and influence some dramatists. "In short, a modern manager need not produce The Wild Duck; but he must be very careful not to produce a play which will seem insipid and old-fashioned to playgoers who have seen The Wild Duck, even though they may have hissed it" (I, 165).

In an important appendix to *The Quintessence of Ibsenism* which appeared only in the first edition, Shaw stated his doubts that actors could perform Ibsen adequately even if the managers were finally to overcome their reluctance to do his plays. For in Ibsen's plays there are few conventional villains and heroes. This accorded well with Shaw's belief that it was perfectly ordinary people who performed the good and evil of the world and not angels and demons. But he felt that the actors of his day were so thoroughly trained to the old school of drama in which the good were very good and the bad horrid that they would not be able to escape from the crude characteristics of old-fashioned stage types. "The more experienced he is, the more certain is he to de-Ibsenize the play into a melodrama or a farcical comedy of the common sort."[2]

Before examining Shaw's treatment of Ibsen in his *Saturday Review* articles, a compact account of the criticisms which have been leveled against Shaw's interpretation of Ibsen, as well as a defense against these criticisms, would be helpful. Critics as diverse as William Archer and Edmund Wilson have charged that Shaw turned Ibsen into a mere polemicist, a peddler of ideas without any poetic importance.[3] Miriam Franc quotes Archer as writing: "A grave injustice has been done Ibsen of late by those of his English admirers who have set him up as a social prophet, and sometimes omitted to mention that he is a bit of a poet as well. . . . People have heard so much of the 'gospel according to Ibsen' that they have come to think of him as a mere hot-gospeller."[4] Sen Gupta takes exception to Shaw's descriptions of Ibsen as prophet and social reformer, and he is right to the extent that Ibsen, according to his own remarks on the subject, was not primarily interested in producing a didactic art work or in playing the role of a propagandist. Furthermore, Sen Gupta finds in Ibsen a mystic element which Shaw chose to ignore. "It is the mystic who moans with Oswald Alving for the sun, who with Hedvig is fascinated by the Wild Duck, who with Thea visualizes Eilert with the vine leaves, and who with Ellida longs for Beauty, Nature, and the Infinite and the Unknown."[5] There is an amusing little quotation from a speech which Ibsen made in 1898 to the Norwegian Society for the Woman's Cause which supports Sen Gupta's picture of Ibsen as relatively unconcerned with social reform: "I thank you for drinking my health, but I must reject the honour of having consciously worked for the woman's cause. I am not even clear what the woman's cause really is. For me it has been an affair of humanity."[6] And yet the woman's cause and humanity are perhaps not different matters after all.

Only recently, two excellent defenses of Shaw have appeared, which serve to set these criticisms in a different light. Both John Gassner and Daniel Charles Gerould[7] distinguish between Ibsen and "Shaw's Ibsen," but illuminatingly point out that "Shaw's Ibsen" usually refers to the views Shaw had during his early Fabian period when he wrote *The Quintessence*, which in fact grew out of some of Shaw's lectures to the Fabian Society. Gassner reminds us that in *The Quintessence of Ibsenism* Shaw takes care to tell us that he is not principally concerned with Ibsen's poetic beauties but, rather, with a consistent theme in Ibsen's plays. Of course, the fact that Shaw told the Fabians, in 1890, that Ibsen was a socialist, which resulted in a newspaper reply from Ibsen denying any partisan associations, only tended to confirm the view that Shaw distorted Ibsen, as Archer had claimed. But both Gassner and Gerould observe that there are three periods of Ibsen criticism in Shaw's writings: the Fabian period, just mentioned, which is avowedly one-sided in its thematic attention to Ibsen; the *Saturday Review* period, in which "since Shaw is now writing practical dramatic criticism, he must perforce deal with plays as plays—and consider the form of the plays and the meaning this form has";[8] and the period of the prefaces to Shaw's own plays, in which he looked back on Ibsen as an old master who actually had limitations. "In the first stage," Gassner observes, "Shaw writes as a

Fabian reformer; in the second, as a journalist reviewer; in the third, as a critic and historian of the drama."[9] Also, according to Gerould, in the Fabian period Shaw was aiming to interest the novel-reading public in the plays of Ibsen, which they were not likely to see on the stage, and so he played down the dramatic and poetic qualities of the plays. Gerould contrasts the treatment of *Peer Gynt* in *The Quintessence*—abstract and ideological—with the treatment of the Paris production of 1896 in the *Saturday Review*—"full of concrete detail and vivid realization of character and situation, and shows an unusual understanding and appreciation of the symbolism."[10] Still later, in the prefaces, Shaw is critical of the accidents, the melodrama, and the morbidity found in many of Ibsen's plays.

The moral earnestness of Ibsen's plays seconded well Shaw's belief in the sacred function of the theater. If the theater is not essentially a place to which people go to be titillated (but only accidentally, because the managers insist on providing titillation), then the fare which is offered should profoundly edify the higher faculties of the audience. Nowhere does Shaw state this more eloquently than in his review, "Ibsen Ahead": "How we have put off the torture of Little Eyolf as one puts off a visit to the dentist. But the torture tempts us in spite of ourselves," and Elizabeth Robins "bids us not only prepare to be tortured, but subscribe to enable her to buy the rack" (II, 240). But this is an agreeable kind of torture, a pleasant ripping off of veils. To know is to be miserable, but, after all, one cannot will not to know; for there is a sort of joyous agony to be obtained from knowledge and though it may be folly to be wise, who can resist entertaining such foolishness? In the review, "Ibsen Triumphant,"

Shaw wrote: "Where shall I find an epithet magnificent enough for The Wild Duck! To sit there getting deeper and deeper into that Ekdal home, and getting deeper and deeper into your own life all the time, until you forget that you are in a theatre; to look on with horror and pity at a profound tragedy, shaking with laughter all the time at an irresistible comedy; to go out, not from a diversion, but from an experience deeper than real life ever brings to most men, or often brings to any man: that is what The Wild Duck was like last Monday at the Globe" (III, 138).

Then, says Shaw, Ibsen succeeds in the function of a serious dramatist: he is saving his audience, he is like the angel of the Annunciation. And when he has serious business at hand, when he is making his audience feel remorse for something they have done or intend to do, he does not need to "entertain" them. Thus, all the tricks of dramatic "construction" become unnecessary once the aim of the dramatist is no longer to entertain (Essays, p. 145). "In the theatre of Ibsen we are not flattered spectators killing an idle hour with an ingenious and amusing entertainment: we are 'guilty creatures sitting at a play' " (Essays, p. 146). The quotation from Hamlet is surely apt; according to Shaw's view of the drama we are all like Claudius, beholding in dramatic effigy the reality of our sins.

This reality is made plain to us by means of the novel device of the Ibsen and post-Ibsen play: the discussion. The discussion resembles a sermon aimed at the consciences of the listeners. Since the listeners are thus involved, even morally incriminated, they become, in a sense, the persons of the drama. A forensic technique replaces the "construction" of the well-made play (Essays, p. 146).

Shaw's consistent use of religious terminology in connection with the theater of Ibsen is no accident: the drama must achieve "scriptural rank," and for this drama is needed the equivalent of an Established Church. This results in the concluding chapter of Shaw's book on Ibsen—a plea for an endowed theater for the performance of Ibsen and other serious modern drama, which would do for the drama what Bayreuth did for Wagnerian opera. For as long as the drama rests in the hands of commercial people who must make money, the drama will have no status as a major art form capable of producing "conviction of sin" in its audience.

If it was the seriousness and didacticism of Ibsen that Shaw admired, what in particular are the elements of Ibsen drama which produced these qualities? To begin with, Shaw looked at the plays as tragicomedies, as we can see from his raptures over *The Wild Duck*. To him, a tragicomedy is a more serious form than tragedy, for it represents daily life much more accurately, by avoiding the posturings of tragic heroes and by avoiding finales of finality. For if in real life there are no finales, the serious but ironic attitude of tragicomedy is more suited to represent such life. "In the new plays, the drama arises through a conflict of unsettled ideals. . . . The conflict is not between clear right and wrong. . . . the question which makes the play interesting . . . is which is the villain and which the hero. . . . there are no villains and no heroes" (*Essays*, p. 139). This marks what Shaw thought of as a return to nature—that things are grey rather than black and white. By tragicomedy, then, Shaw means a form in which there is little that is decisive, definite, final. There is no clear villain, no clear catastrophe; life and its problems go on.

The originality of the "discussion" in Ibsen's plays is somewhat exaggerated by Shaw, as is the frequency of its appearance. That Ibsen had escaped at all from the machinery of the well-made play was enough to produce an immoderate enthusiasm in Shaw for the elements which marked the escape. In *The Quintessence of Ibsenism*, Shaw traces Ibsen's gradual departure from the old methods of "construction." He sees in *The League of Youth* "an ingenious comedy of intrigue, clever enough in its mechanical construction to entitle the French to claim that Ibsen owes something to his technical education . . . in the school of Scribe" (*Essays*, p. 62). Of *A Doll's House* Shaw observed that the omission of a few lines here and there and the substitution of a happy ending would have yielded a well-made play. But the discussion saves it, for at the critical moment in the last act, "the heroine very unexpectedly . . . stops her emotional acting and says: 'We must sit down and discuss all this' " (*Essays*, p. 138). Elsewhere Shaw says that Ibsen's "elaborate gradual development" would have satisfied Dumas (*Essays*, p. 110). But even though Ibsen emancipated himself somewhat from stagey tragedy, from "construction," and from entertaining happy endings, Shaw did not feel that he had quite escaped from fifth-act blank-verse conclusions:

For perhaps the most plausible reproach levelled at Ibsen by modern critics of his own school is just that survival of the old school in him which makes the death rate so high in his last acts. Do Oswald Alving, Hedvig Ekdal, Rosmer and Rebecca, Hedda Gabler, Solness, Eyolf, Borkman, Rubeck and Irene die dramatically natural deaths, or are they slaughtered in the classic and Shakespearean manner, partly because the audience expects blood for its money, partly because it is difficult to make people attend seriously to anything except by startling them with some violent calamity? It is so easy to make out a case for either view that I shall not argue the point. (*Essays*, p. 142)

But at least the deaths are not accidents and are not there mainly as a reason for the play's existing, as they seemed to Shaw to be in the plays of Shakespeare.

In connection with the deaths in Ibsen and with his use of discussion, one feels that Shaw is often speaking more about his own plays than Ibsen's. For example, regarding the discussion, Shaw remarks that since *A Doll's House* "the discussion has expanded far beyond the limits of the last ten minutes of an otherwise 'well made' play" (*Essays*, p. 138), but one is inclined to ask, Where but in Shaw's own plays is this found to be the case? One thinks of *Man and Superman* especially, though virtually any Shaw play will do. Possibly, as Sen Gupta argues, Shaw generalizes too rashly when he says: "The action of such [modern] plays consists of a case to be argued. . . . the play in which there is no argument and no case no longer counts as serious drama" (*Essays*, p. 139). Indeed, Gassner makes the point that the "drama of ideas was to a considerable degree Shaw's contribution to dramatic theory; it was, in part, a Shavian discovery and, in part, a Shavian invention useful in the struggle for liberal principles and modern social drama."[11]

Discussion, minimal "construction," deaths that are not accidental, attempts to deal with daily life— these are some of the formal differences between older drama (whether Shakespearean or Pinerotic) and Ibsen drama. But the essential difference is in the increased moral awareness of the Ibsen plays. Although in Ibsen the morality is more dramatized than discussed (whereas in Shaw it is more discussed), it is dramatized without romance, and this absence of romance Shaw finds congenial. Ibsen's personae are from the middle class; they are architects, businessmen, or judges rather than aristocrats. They are suburban, representing what Shaw called "the genteel slums" (II, 257). What we are shown is their guilty conscience, especially in marriage, for marriage is a modern subject —older literature dealt with courtship and romance. In displaying the closeted skeletons of marriage to the world, Ibsen was presenting the audience with the life of their own time, freed from romanticism and literariness. In many of his reviews of plays not by Ibsen, Shaw complains that human life as treated on the stage gradually became a set of fantastic conventions which had little relation to life as it is lived. When people went to the theater, any picture of life which was not composed of these stage conventions seemed unreal. Thus the reality of the stage and the reality of real life came to have little in common. By eliminating, or at least altering, these conventional representations of life, Ibsen appeared to Shaw a realist, as opposed to the romanticist who finds that the only "natural" way to end a play is to strew the stage with bloody bodies.

In addition to being idealistic, Ibsen did not feel obliged to be pleasing—to "be agreeable to Tom, Dick, and Harry" (III, 30). To "enjoy" Ibsen requires a strong mind—one might almost say to enjoy Ibsen requires a Shavian mind, a mind that can bear much reality. Since the average man cannot bear much reality, he is not pleased, said Shaw, by the view of nature "as seen under Ibsen rays that pierce our most secret cupboards and reveal the grin of the skeleton there" (II, 241). To Shaw, this grinning skeleton was particularly welcome because it rebelled against the effects of Robertsonian drama which were still felt in the nineties: a tailor's mannequin making love to a milliner's model, both looking very respectable. "The stockbrokerly young gentleman, standing on the stage with his manners carefully turned to the audience . . . has suddenly been taken by the scruff of the neck by the grim Norwegian giant, and, with one ruthless twist, whisked round with his seamy side to the footlights. . . . The drawing room comedy of furniture and manners, with a tastefully conducted intrigue as a pretext, is as dead as Donizetti and deader" (I, 279). Ibsen's characters just will not keep up appearances. They have a compulsion to open those closets that are fatal to their reputed respectability. This compulsion causes them to come out not only with their own guilty secrets, but with ours too (*Pen Portraits*, p. 142).

Shaw found that the critics could not bear the Ibsen realities:

In John Gabriel Borkman . . . a lady, Mrs Wilton, elopes with a young man. Being a woman of some experience, thoroughly alive to the possibility that she will get tired of the young man, or the young man of her, not to mention the certainty of their boring one another if they are left alone together too much with no resource but lovemaking, she takes the precaution of bringing another woman along with her. This incident has provoked a poignant squeal of indignation from the English Press. . . . we could not stand Mrs Wilton's forethought. . . . But please observe that if Ibsen had represented Mrs Wilton as finding a love letter addressed by Borkman Junior to Frida Feldal, and as having thereupon murdered them both and then slain herself in despair on their corpses, everybody would have agreed that a lady could do no less, and that Ibsen had shewn the instinct of a true tragic poet in inventing the incident. (III, 61)

As far as Shaw could see, the critics were addicted to the romantic conventions of the stage as much as anybody.

The great feature of Ibsen's morality, by happy coincidence, is the Shaw-Schopenhauer dictum that man is ruled by a will which he justifies by reason; such justification of irrationality puts the rational faculties in a grim light. According to the theory of will, a man first decides what he wants and then uses his reason to prove to himself and the world that what he has just decided irrationally is evidently the best course to follow. Though it is not likely that Ibsen wrote his plays to dramatize *The World as Will and Idea*, Shaw nevertheless was convinced that the Schopenhauerian doctrine was implicit in the Ibsen canon. Ibsen knew, he remarks, that men do not act according to principles but merely justify their actions according to principles. The quintessence of Ibsen is that there is no formula: "What Ibsen insists on is that there is no golden rule; that conduct must justify itself by its effect upon life and not by its conformity to any rule or ideal" (*Essays*, p. 125). The Ibsenist solution is that there is no solution (II, 253). Then, too, if all progress depends on the overturning of old institutions and beliefs, rules cannot be very useful guides, for they cannot remain unchanged for long. (Often Shaw's doctrine of progress calls to mind Carlyle's notion of customs and institutions as the attire of the spirit—an attire which wears out like any other and must be replaced with new.) "All religions begin with a revolt against morality. . . . Ibsen's attack on morality is a symptom of the revival of religion, not of its extinction" (*Essays,* p. 121). Note how characteristically Shavian is Shaw's description of what lies behind the Ibsen morality: "He protests against the ordinary assumption that there are certain moral institutions which justify all means used to maintain them, and insists that the supreme end shall be the inspired, eternal, ever growing one, not the external unchanging, artificial one" (*Essays,* p. 122). There is great self-restraint in his reluctance to come right out with it and call it the Life Force.

The "inspired, eternal, ever growing end" which Shaw talks about is the increased intellectual self-awareness brought about by the Life Force. This increase is hampered by conventional morality and conventional notions of truth. The avenue to greater personal and racial self-consciousness is fulfillment of the individual will, which requires the self-confidence necessary to rely on the essential rightness of one's own will. If one's will lacks essential rightness, if one is not, in other words, Dick Dudgeon or John Tanner, one is pretty hopeless. In the Shavian system of things, if one is not a member of the elect one had best pack up and leave. Precisely where one goes is a problem Shaw resigns to those who must go.

Shaw was able to see inspired glimmerings of the philosophy of Will and Creative Evolution in Ibsen, and since he had his own axe to grind he perhaps found Ibsen to be more Shavian than he actually was. When he describes the moral imperative behind the Ibsen plays as, "let everyone religiously refuse to sacrifice himself and others from the moment he loses his faith in the validity of the ideal" (*Essays*, p. 123), one is sure one has heard that tune before but less sure that it comes from Ibsen.

The Shavian reliance on Will instead of legality and conventionality (Dick Dudgeon vs. Mrs. Dudgeon) is a modern version of the Pauline antithesis of faith and law. Instead of faith we now have Will. The following passage from *The Quintessence of Ibsenism* is the story of *The Devil's Disciple:*

The respectable lady of the strictest Church principles, who has brought up her children with such relentless regard to their ideal morality that if they have any spirit left in them by the time they arrive at years of independence they use their liberty to rush deliriously to the devil: this unimpeachable woman has always felt it unjust that the respect she wins should be accompanied by deep-seated detestation, whilst the latest spiritual heiress of Nell Gwynne, whom no respectable person dare bow to in the street, is a popular idol. The reason is—though the idealist lady does not know it— that Nell Gwynne is a better woman than she. (*Essays*, p. 124)

Moral evolution to Shaw was the continual repudiation of duty. (I do not recall reading any comments by Shaw on Kant's ethics, but he surely must have detested them.) First the duty to God must be renounced, then to man (i.e., social conventions). One must come to be true to oneself. Men who shatter the old superstitions are the realists, whereas men who create superstitions to protect them from the truth of their own natures are the idealists. Each age requires a realist to destroy the lies of the previous age. In some of the Ibsen plays, there is a character who stands against popular opinion and becomes a realist-martyr. In other plays, the realist is Ibsen himself, who stands behind the characters and exposes their hypocrisy by means of dramatic conflict. Thus, as Shaw reads it, in *A Doll's House* we have the old superstition of "A woman's place is in the home" exposed, partly through Nora herself. In *An Enemy of the People* we have commercial ethics exposed. And so on. Someone sees through the words into the realities and an exposure of the vice behind respectability inevitably follows. Shaw's description of the nature of idealists—that is, people who disguise vice in beautiful words and arresting images—is worth quoting at length:

For the sake of precision, let us imagine a community of a thousand persons, organized for the perpetuation of the species on the basis of the British family as we know it at present. Seven hundred of them, we will suppose, find the British family arrangement quite good enough for them. Two hundred and ninety-nine find it a failure, but must put up with it since they are in a minority. The remaining person occupies a position to be explained presently. The 299 failures will not have the courage to face the fact that they are irremediable failures, since they cannot prevent the 700 satisfied ones from coercing them into conformity with the marriage law. They will accordingly try to persuade themselves that, whatever their own particular domestic arrangements may be, the family is a beautiful and holy natural institution. For the fox not only declares that the grapes he cannot get are sour: he also insists that the sloes he can get are sweet. Now observe what has happened. The family as it really is is a conventional arrangement, legally enforced, which the majority, because it happens to suit them, think good enough for the minority, whom it happens not to suit at all. The family as a beautiful and holy natural institution is only a fancy picture of what every family would have to be if everybody was to be suited, invented by the minority as a mask for the reality, which in its nakedness is intolerable to them. We call this sort of fancy picture an Ideal; and the policy of forcing individuals to act on the assumption that all ideals are real, and to recognize and accept such action as standard moral conduct, absolutely valid under all circumstances, contrary conduct or any advocacy of it being discountenanced and punished as immoral, may therefore be described as the policy of Idealism. Our 299 domestic failures are therefore become idealists as to marriage; and in proclaiming the ideal in fiction, poetry, pulpit and platform oratory, and serious private conversation, they will far outdo the 700 who comfortably accept marriage as a matter of course, never dreaming of calling it an "institution," much less a holy and beautiful one, and being pretty plainly of opinion that Idealism is a crackbrained fuss about nothing. The idealists, hurt by this, will retort by calling them Philistines. We then have our society classified as 700 Philistines and 299 idealists, leaving one man unclassified: the man strong enough to face the truth the idealists are shirking. (*Essays*, pp. 26-27)

When this realist speaks against marriage and exposes its defects, the populace think him mad and the idealists hate him. They will crucify him and regard him as immoral and foul. He, of course, is the Shaw-Ibsen hero. "We are now prepared to learn without misgiving that a typical Ibsen play is one in which the leading lady is an unwomanly woman, and the villain an idealist" (*Essays*, p. 42).

The Quintessence of Ibsenism, after its preliminary discussions about idealists and society, goes on to trace these general themes within the plays, plays which were "written by Ibsen to illustrate his thesis that the real slavery of today is slavery to ideals of goodness" (*Essays*, p. 117). Shaw explains that Peer Gynt and Brand are idealists who care more about their castles in the air than castles of brick and mortar. Brand is so concerned with things as they ought to be that he becomes a monster of inhumanity, whereas Peer suffers from the illusion that his will can overcome everything and as a result he loses touch with the real world. In *Emperor and Galilean,* another poetic drama, Shaw found his philosophy of Will dramatized in the Emperor Julian's inability to grasp the idea that there was no power above him and outside of him which could solve his dilemmas or provide moral strength. "He had felt the godhead in himself, but not in others. Being only able to say, with half conviction, 'The kingdom of heaven is within ME,' he had been utterly vanquished by the Galilean who had been able to say, 'The kingdom of heaven is within YOU.' But he was on the way to that full truth. A man cannot believe in others until he believes in himself; for his conviction of the equal worth of his fellows must be filled by the overflow of his conviction of his own worth" (*Essays*, p. 58).

What is unusual about the Ibsen "villains" is that they are the people who would be heroes in "conventional" literature. For to be a Shaw-Ibsen villain, it is necessary to be intelligent enough and imaginative enough to have grandiose notions. A certain thick-headedness prevents such men, however, from being real heroes. "Brand and Rosmer, who drive those they love to death, do so with all the fine airs of the Sophoclean or Shakespearean good man persecuted by destiny" (*Essays*, p. 118).

It was Ibsen's middle period which produced both the strongest public reaction in England and Shaw's best criticism. Perhaps the most famous reaction of all is the one Shaw liked so much to quote—Clement Scott's remarkable horror over the presentation of *Ghosts* in March, 1891. Scott is represented by Shaw as an important figure in the drama of the days of Robertson but superannuated in the era of Ibsen. He suffered from a number of disadvantages as far as Shaw was concerned—he was sentimentally good-natured, Roman Catholic, and emotionally excitable. He described *Ghosts* as "an open drain; a loathsome sore unbandaged; a dirty act done publicly," and achieved thereby a measure of immortality as Shaw's classic example of unenlightened middle-class respectability —that is, an idealist:

But Clement Scott's criticism was hardly distinguishable in tone from dozens of others which appeared simultaneously. His opinion was the vulgar opinion. . . . For example, in Ghosts, the play in question, a clergyman and a married woman fall in love with one another. The woman proposes to abandon her husband and live with the clergyman. He recalls her to her duty, and makes her behave as a virtuous woman. She afterwards tells him that this was a crime on his part. Ibsen agrees with her, and has written the play to bring you round to his opinion. Clement Scott did not agree with her, and believed that when you are brought round to her opinion you have been morally corrupted. By this conviction he was impelled to denounce Ibsen as he did, Ibsen being equally impelled to propagate the convictions which provoked the attack. Which of the two is right cannot be decided until it is ascertained whether a society of persons holding Ibsen's opinions would be higher or lower than a society holding Clement Scott's. (*Essays*, pp. 15-17)

It is interesting to recall that what is at heart the same situation arises in *The Devil's Disciple* when Annie Dudgeon is advised by Parson Hawkins not to marry a socially condemned Life Forcer whom she loves, but to marry instead a piously respectable man whom she does not love. The same reproach is made at the end of Shaw's play as at the end of Ibsen's.

A *Doll's House* is something of a landmark in the drama, for, besides having a discussion at the end, the play appears to deal with a modern social problem, even though Ibsen has confessed his innocence of the charge in the speech quoted above. Miriam Franc quotes a similar Ibsen disclaimer: "Whatever I have written has been without any conscious thought of making propaganda. I have been more poet and less social philosopher than people generally seem inclined to believe. . . . My task has been the description of humanity."[12] To Shaw, Nora's slamming the door was like a modern shot heard around the world. "Nora's departure is no clap-trap 'Farewell for ever,' but a journey in search of self-respect and apprenticeship to life. . . . Nora's revolt is the end of a chapter of human history" (III, 130-31). Shaw appreciated perhaps too much the emancipation of Nora from woman's inferior status, because only when women are given a chance to be on an equal footing with men can one feel contempt for their inferiority without qualms of injustice. Shaw's conscience, then, could be clear. His remark that "the domestic career is no more natural to all

women than the military career is natural to all men"
(*Essays*, pp. 38-39) at least leaves an opening for his
genuine appreciation of intellectual women who, very
likely, wore "rational dress," to use his phrase. (One
must consider that Ann Whitefield, for all her triumph
in *Man and Superman* and for all her fulfillment of
the energies of the Life Force, is really the object of a
Shavian sneer. For Shaw's admiration of the blinder
and more sensual energies of the Life Force was always
a nervous one. Sex is better than "piety," but platonic
spirituality is what he really preferred.) The notion of
a Womanly Woman is just another of man's idealist
inventions whose purpose is to make the less-than-
satisfactory reality into a beautiful illusion. Whether
the Unwomanly Woman is anything better than a
poor specimen of a man is an open question. For if in
fact even in modern society neither women nor men
really want women to be precisely equal to men,
women appear to remain as much a problem as ever,
even after Shaw disposed of them.

In his discussion of *The Wild Duck* he develops
one of his major ideas—that external codes do not
change the person and that every choice and every act
is a new one that must be determined afresh. The traditions which have been built up over the centuries are
probably necessary for the multitude, but a person of
intelligence must live a life *ab ovo*. "All you can
wisely do is to remove what you can of the external
obstacles . . . and then wait for the operation of his
internal impulse. . . . If he has no such impulse, then
you must put up with him as he is" (*Essays*, p. 78). If
you chance to be Dick Dudgeon, you are in luck. If
you chance to be Roebuck Ramsden, one must take
you as you are. The future looks almost as bleak as the

past, for Shaw's view is ultimately a Hegelian one in which civilization is an evolution from thesis to antithesis to the synthesis which is soon to be a new thesis. This means that civilization is the unrolling of a drama in which martyrs and philistines are the chief personages. Shaw as a martyr can lash out against the philistines, knowing that for his own age, at least, he is on the side of the angels. But the pattern must unfold forever in the same way, with no hope of permanent victory, for today's martyrs are tomorrow's philistines. The only hope lies in the fact that tomorrow's philistines are as enlightened as today's martyrs.

The "progress" which Shaw finds in Ibsen's dramas, but which is less disputably present in his own, can be seen very well in his contrasting of the "old school," typified by Dickens, with the new school of Ibsen and Strindberg. In "old school" literature there are funny characters and underdogs, who are treated as if they were not full human beings like the "good" people. But "there is not one of Ibsen's characters who is not . . . the temple of the Holy Ghost. . . . The Dickens-Thackeray spirit is, in comparison, that of a Punch and Judy showman, who is never restrained from whacking his little figures unmercifully by the sense that they, too, are images of God" (*Essays*, p. 131). In modern literature like Ibsen's there are no good or bad characters, no heroes or villains—there are not even serious or comic characters. All of the characters are treated like members of the same species, members who are not motivated by narrow humors and non-human consistencies. "No character drawn by Dickens is more ridiculous than Hjalmar Ekdal in The Wild Duck, . . . and yet these Ekdals wring the heart

whilst Micawber and Chivery . . . only shake the sides"
(*Essays*, pp. 131-32).

Ibsen, then, was an early martyr of the age, who
gave many indications of being a battler against the
philistines. He challenged old assumptions and turned
them into new questions. He was a step ahead in the
progress of self-consciousness, which is the main aim
of the Life Force. But he was to Shaw only a John the
Baptist heralding a new Messiah, who would soon be
the author of *Man and Superman*.

Chapter 6

THE CENSORSHIP

SHAW WAS one of those rare people whose public life and private life (insofar as we know it) show a consistent adherence to the same principles. Reading his plays, his prefaces, his tracts, his letters, one is struck by the unusual degree to which the same person is present everywhere. Whether he was preaching to Mrs. Campbell in a "love letter" or fulminating against the censor in a public document, it was always the same Shaw. But nowhere is Shaw's candor more evident, more flagrant, more outrageous, than in his scourging of the Examiner of Plays.

The censorship of the stage began during the time of Walpole as a measure to prevent men like Fielding and Gay from exposing parliamentary corruption by means of so public a medium as the drama. Plays, political tracts, pamphlets, satires, and burlesques were written to criticize Walpole and his Whig ministry. Among the dramas, Gay's *The Beggar's Opera*, *Polly*, and Cibber's *Love in a Riddle* are a few of the more familiar works.[1] By the Act of 1737, the Lord Chamberlain was empowered to give or withhold licenses for individual plays, and thus began what amounted to a one-man despotism over the theater. The objections against such an institution are, naturally, innumerable, and in the course of his lifetime Shaw probably stated as many as anybody. Happily, his many years of effort to abolish the office of the Examiner were not entirely in vain, although the office still exists.

The Examiner, as a member of the king's household, is not elected to office, nor does he have to qualify himself by means of any examinations. Thus, if he is not particularly intelligent, the drama will necessarily suffer greatly. Before the parliamentary investigation of 1909, at which time the power of the censor was made less subject to a single individual and his limitations, this "unenlightened despotism," as Shaw called it, prevented many serious plays from reaching the stage. Shaw described the procedure as follows: "You take a commonplace official; confront him with a play by a man probably cleverer than himself . . . and ask him to decide whether the net effect of a performance of that play on the destiny of the human race will be helpful or harmful. The Delphic oracle itself would not have the impudence to pretend that it could answer such a question."[2] Doubtless, when Shaw wrote these words he had in mind his own battles with the Examiner. But he was also interested in the status of the drama itself and throughout his criticism for the *Saturday Review* had campaigned vigorously for the emancipation of the drama. His feuds with Mr. Pigott and Mr. Redford come immediately to mind and especially his triumphant article on the death of Mr. Pigott in 1895, which Shaw referred to as "the most abusive article ever written on a recently dead man":[3]

Mr E. F. Smyth Pigott, for twenty years examiner of stage plays to the Lord Chamberlain's department, has joined the majority. . . . The justification of the Censorship is to be found in the assumption . . . that, if the stage were freed, managers would immediately produce licentious plays; actresses would leave off clothing themselves decently; and the public would sit nightly wallowing in the obscenity which the Censor now sternly withholds from them. This assumption evidently involves the further one, that the Examiner of Plays is so much better than his neighbors, as to be untainted by their assumed love of filth. This is where the theory of the Censorship breaks down in practice. The Lord Chamberlain's reader is not selected by examination either in literature or morals. His emoluments, estimated at about £800 a year, will fetch nothing more in the market than well connected mediocrity. Therefore it is necessary to give him absolute power, so that there may be no appeal from his blunders. If he vetoes serious plays and licenses nasty ones, which is exactly what the late Mr Pigott did, there is no remedy. (I, 48)

The article goes on to chastise Mr. Pigott in particular —and the result is virtually a summary of Shaw's anti-censorship campaign: "The late Mr Pigott is declared on all hands to have been the best reader of plays we have ever had; and yet he was a walking compendium of vulgar insular prejudice. . . . He had French immorality on the brain; he had American indecency on the brain; he had the womanly woman on the brain; he had the Divorce Court on the brain; he had 'not before a mixed audience' on the brain" (I, 49).

Shaw had seen, only a few weeks before Pigott's death, the play *A Leader of Men*, by Charles Ward, which he regarded as potentially instructive historical comedy that had been altered with the censorship in mind. He then raised the question: What would this play have been like without the censorship looming overhead? "Mr Ward, like all dramatic authors, has had to choose between infanticide and abortion; and he has chosen abortion. . . . Probably there is not a playwright in the country who has not thought of giving artistic life and form to that drama, only to relinquish the project at the thought of Mr Pigott, and to pass on, possibly, to some farcical comedy theme sufficiently salacious to be sure of a license" (I, 37).

The evil that Pigott did was certainly not interred with his bones, for Shaw's little requiem on Pigott underscores it with Dickensian gusto: "It is a frightful thing to see the greatest thinkers, poets, and authors of modern Europe . . . delivered helpless into the vulgar hands of such a noodle as this amiable old gentleman—this despised and incapable old official—most notoriously was" (I, 54). Would Shakespeare or the Greek dramatists have had a chance with Mr. Pigott? No—and the only reason *they* are allowed on the stage, Shaw noted, is that they existed before the licensing act was born.

Shaw has preserved a statement which Pigott made on the plays of Ibsen: " 'I have studied Ibsen's plays pretty carefully; and all the characters in Ibsen's plays appear to me morally deranged. All the heroines are dissatisfied spinsters who look on marriage as a monopoly, or dissatisfied married women in a chronic state of rebellion against not only the conditions which nature has imposed on their sex, but against all the duties and obligations of mothers and wives. As for the men, they are all rascals or imbeciles' " (I, 52-53). Clement Scott, at least, would have agreed!

Shaw repeatedly notes that the Examiner cannot tell a good play from a bad—and if he could, the stage would probably become a political weapon of the party in power—that is, it would do the very thing which the censorship was set up to prevent. Two consequences of the modest intellectual powers of the Examiner are, Shaw asserted, that no really serious author in England cares to write plays at all, because he would have to write them down to the level of the Examiner, and that the stage loses its power as a means of social reform, because such serious issues—or indeed any matters which challenge accepted opinions—are invariably blue-penciled by the Examiner. According to a recent writer on censorship of the drama, the banning of the plays of Brieux in England "was clearly a strong deterrent to English authors to express any . . . strong and high moral views in their own plays."[4] Shaw, furthermore, claimed that the censorship undoubtedly prevented many plays from being written altogether.

Submitting a play to the Examiner involved a fee of several guineas. If the play was acceptable, it was thenceforth and forever free from any further obligations. Originally, if it was unacceptable, the objectionable passages were pointed out and the author could adjust them and resubmit the play along with a second payment. But in Shaw's day the Examiner would no longer point out the offensive passages; he would merely state that the play was unacceptable and leave the author to determine the grievance. Shaw regarded this as a guessing game aimed at earning more money for the Examiner. "This meant that if I would guess the obnoxious passages, and send him another ten dollars and a half, he would tell me whether my guess was right."[5]

What is surprising is that the protests against the censorship were not universal and that the Examiner was even defended. In one of his *Saturday Review* articles Shaw quarrels with Clement Scott for actually praising the censorship. And when he looks back on the struggle years later, Shaw is able to point to his own articles as among the chief forces against the abuses of the censorship. The aim which lies behind all of those articles is to render the stage as free as the press. For all kinds of injustice are involved in the office of Examiner: the mind of the particular man in office becomes the measure of all things; the decisions, unlike court decisions which depend on a jury, are made by one man—whose qualifications are dubious; the grounds for the decision remain secret: "A playwright's livelihood, his reputation . . . are at the personal mercy of the Censor. The two do not stand, as the criminal and the judge stand, in the presence of a law that binds them both equally. . . . The only law that affects them is the Act of 1843, which empowers one of them to do absolutely and finally what he likes with the other's work" (*Prefaces*, p. 416).

What did the Examiner actually allow to pass and what did he forbid and why? It is a remarkable fact that he allowed obscene and pornographic plays to pass onto the stage while refusing licenses to serious plays like *Ghosts* and *Mrs. Warren's Profession*. The cause is fairly clear: the Examiner was the champion of middle-class morality, that is, of pious hypocrisy. Anything that might undermine conventional beliefs was unacceptable. The very hypocrisies which Ibsen exposed in his plays were practiced by the Examiner in banning Ibsen's plays—and Shaw's. Furthermore, no play that attacked government officials was permissible, no quotations from Scripture, no irreverence, no incest or unconventional sex, no unreformed sexual promiscuity (all the ladies with pasts have a very sad time of it in their later years). On the other hand, "plenty of fun and a happy ending will get anything licensed, because the public will have it so" (*Prefaces*, p. 419). What Shaw found particularly immoral was that vice was always seen on the stage to have happy consequences. A play could be as licentious as it pleased provided there was the equivalent of deathbed repentance at the end. Ironically enough, Mr. Pigott once wrote that the audiences at plays were really quite moral: "A boy might pick your pocket as you left the theatre, but have his reserve of fine sentiment in his heart" (I, 53). That is the mentality Shaw loathed.

Shaw has given us a number of illustrations of the kind of licentiousness which had no trouble passing the Examiner. In one instance, the hero is about to rape the heroine but fails. Shaw points out that if he had succeeded, the play would have been unacceptable. "The present arrangement entertains the public with just as much of a rape as it is possible to present on the stage at all, Censorship or no Censorship" (III, 366). One recalls Richardson's *Pamela*, another paragon of middle-class morality. Mrs. Pamela, her chastity inviolate, undergoes a series of licentious escapades to which a successful rape could have added nothing at all. Fittingly, "divine Richardson" was held up as youth's greatest mentor. The popular mind, as Shaw so well knew, cannot distinguish between the letter and the spirit: as long as you do not succeed in doing what is forbidden, you can try as hard as you can to do it— and still be on the side of the angels: "Adultery and prostitution are tolerated and even encouraged to such an extent that plays which do not deal with them are commonly said not to be plays at all. But if any of the

unpleasing consequences of adultery and prostitution
—for instance, an unsuccessful illegal operation (successful ones are tolerated) or venereal disease—are
mentioned, the play is prohibited" (Prefaces, pp. 419-
20). In order, however, to perform "unacceptable"
plays like The Cenci and Ghosts, the managers must
hire private halls and pretend that the performances
are not public. Indeed, imaginary clubs and subscription series have had to be invented in order to make
some performances possible.

In 1925 Shaw looked back at the theatrical world of
the nineties and of the drama and remarked, "It had
only one subject, which the censorship did not allow it
to mention. Janet Achurch was forbidden to produce a
little play by Octave Feuillet, about a lady with what
we called a past, until she gave the Censor her word of
honor to say every night on the stage, 'I sinned but in
intention,' which she accordingly whispered to the
conductor most faithfully always on her first entry."[6]
It is an amusing society, the society represented by the
Examiner, for, according to its ideals, you can get to
heaven only by works. If you have faith, you go directly to hell.

In connection with the Examiner's disapproval of
Mrs. Warren's Profession, Shaw wrote: "Members of
Mrs Warren's profession shall be tolerated on the stage
only when they are beautiful, exquisitely dressed, and
sumptuously lodged and fed; also . . . they shall, at the
end of the play, die of consumption to the sympathetic tears of the whole audience, or step into the next
room to commit suicide" (Prefaces, pp. 221-22). After
submitting his play, Shaw received a letter from the
Examiner, which read in part: "Most certainly it is not
for me to attempt any 'dramatic expurgation' with the

blue pencil, as you appear to suggest. It is for you to submit, or cause to be submitted, a licensable play, and if you do this I will endeavour to forget that I ever read the original."[7] After Shaw had made revisions, for the sake of public performance only, and received a letter of permission for the new version, he said that the letter was "an insolent and insufferable document, which I cannot read without boiling of the blood, certifying that in his opinion—*his* opinion!—" the play was now acceptable (*Prefaces*, p. 720).

Shaw believed that the managers liked the censorship because once a play was licensed no problem remained. It was a guinea insurance policy, well worth the cost. It was a way of avoiding personal responsibility for the consequences of a public performance, for, after all, if a play was good enough for the Examiner, who would contest it once it had been licensed?

The essence of Shaw's objection to the censorship is actually the issue of the Life Force in another guise. The middle-class morality which animated the censorship was devoted to the principle that anything which shocked "respectable" people was objectionable. But most new ideas which run counter to conventional beliefs are at first shocking. Therefore, most new ideas are objectionable. But Shaw believed in the theater as a modern replacement for the church, as the source of moral enlightenment. Thus his retort to the censorship was: "It is no more possible for me to do my work honestly as a playwright without giving pain than it is for a dentist. The nation's morals are like its teeth: the more decayed they are the more it hurts to touch them" (*Prefaces*, p. 436). The reason why people protest against *Mrs. Warren's Profession* and not against *King Lear* is that Shakespeare's quarrel was not with a

particular social class but with God. If he had quar-
reled with a specific class of people, he would have
been denounced (*Prefaces*, p. 201). "All censorships
exist to prevent anyone from challenging current conceptions and existing institutions. All progress is initi-
ated by challenging current conceptions, and executed
by supplanting existing institutions. Consequently
the first condition of progress is the removal of censorships" (*Prefaces*, p. 226). Instead of *censoring* the
2 per cent of plays in which "received opinions and
hardened prejudices are called in question" (I, 49),
Shaw believed that the Examiner ought to *recommend*
them. But this does not happen, because convention
is like traffic signals. Everyone must agree on what
green means so that people can cross streets without
getting killed. Soon they come to believe that there is
some inherent quality of greenness responsible for going rather than stopping. Any proffered change will
terrify them, because conventions enable people to
know where they stand. To a militant free-willer like
Shaw, however, it is worth sacrificing the security of
knowing where one stands in order to achieve something greater. Once society has a mind to believing,
say, that abortion is monstrous, any attempt to deal
with abortion in a play will be regarded as monstrous
too. Even if the play tries to show that abortion is
monstrous! "If a girl may refer to her virginity on the
stage, what may she not refer to?" (*Prefaces*, p. 211)
Shaw tells a fine anecdote about a Frenchman in Westminster Abbey who was seen to kneel down and pray:

The verger, who had never seen such a thing happen
before, promptly handed him over to the police and
charged him with "brawling." Fortunately, the magistrate had compassion on the foreigner's ignorance; and

even went the length of asking why he should not be allowed to pray in church. The reply of the verger was simple and obvious. "If we allowed that," he said, "we should have people praying all over the place." And to this day the rule in Westminster Abbey is that you may stroll about and look at the monuments; but you must not on any account pray. Similarly, on the stage you may represent murder, gluttony, sexual vice, and all the crimes in the calendar and out of it; but you must not say anything unusual about them. (*Prefaces*, p. 211)

The Examiner may be a dolt, said Shaw, but things would be even worse if he had intelligence. For then he would see the *tendency* of a play and not just what was obvious in it—and then he would censor even more. But even if we allow the Examiner to remain a dolt, he cannot judge the play effectively unless he sees it on the stage. For all kinds of suggestive innuendoes appear in performance which are not discernible in the printed play. Sometimes, in fact, the performance turns an unobjectionable play into a licentious one. But if the Examiner began to judge plays on the basis of performance, he would also have to go to music halls, since virtually everything done there is "performance" rather than "book." This is obviously impossible. The only kind of regulation of the theaters which Shaw approved of and regarded as feasible bore a close resemblance to a pub license: orderliness, not art, was its object. Insofar as any control at all is desirable or possible in connection with plays as art, it should be nothing more than granting or withholding a license to operate a theater. This would make individual managers responsible for the conduct of their theater and would discourage any really obscene plays from being performed.[8] "What, then, is to be done with the Censorship? Nothing can be simpler. Abolish it, root and branch, throwing the whole legal responsibility for plays on the author and manager, precisely as the legal responsibility for a book is thrown on the author, the printer, and the publisher. The managers will not like this: their present slavery is safer and easier; but it will be good for them, and good for the Drama."[9] For all his violent anti-censorship campaigning, Shaw did not have strong hope of abolishing the censorship, because he saw that it was not a political issue and that there were very few interested parties. "The censorship will probably outlive the House of Lords and the supremacy of the Established Church."[10]

R. M. Smith, in his dissertation on modern censorship, describes the ultimate effect which Shaw produced after years of writing against the censorship. Regarding the parliamentary inquiry of 1909 (fully discussed in the preface to *Blanco Posnet*), Smith writes: "Although the report of the Committee failed to recommend the abolition of the official censorship and the institution survived, the Committee gave such strong warning against the possibilities for abuse inherent in the office that the dramatist was practically insured as much freedom as other artists command. . . . As a result of the pre-war [World War I] protests of the dramatic authors, the post-war appointees to the position of Examiner have been men of more culture and background than most of their predecessors."[11] Besides this, the establishment of a standing advisory committee was a means of eliminating the secrecy and tyranny of a one-man Examiner.

Although Shaw did not succeed in getting rid of the office of Examiner altogether, he did succeed in making its power more closely resemble the power of the House of Lords.

Chapter 7

ACTORS AND ACTING

As the Victorian theater expanded in size, the style of acting tended to broaden along with it, for niceties of execution could not be clearly seen or heard from a distance. In addition, there was a tendency in the dramatists to write stock characterizations into their plays, not only because an old success was very likely to be a new success when put into a new play, but because a stock character could be grasped by the audience even under the adverse conditions of the large theater.[1]

When Shaw remarked that "dramatic authorship has become the art of exploiting the personalities of popular favorites" (I, 223), he voiced one of his most frequent complaints against the theater. For the theater suffers from an irremediable conflict between the literary and the histrionic. When the dramatists are men of literature and artistic integrity, it is difficult for the actors to indulge their exhibitionist impulses irresponsibly. But when the dramatists are mediocre timeservers, the plays become mere vehicles and occasions for ballet-style displays of acting. There is, of course, a large audience available for such displays, but to a critic who was also an intellectual dramatist, such an audience and the actors who catered to it and the dramatists who catered to the actors seemed irresponsible. In regarding the theater as a sacred place where the soul could be made more and more aware of itself, Shaw was like a prophet who chased moneylenders from the temple.

Except for his criticisms of Irving and Tree, Shaw's pronouncements on acting are directed mainly at actresses. In view of his ambivalent attitudes toward women, Shaw's remarks about actresses are laden with tremors of repulsion and attraction. For as Chesterton has keenly observed, Shaw's mania for the emancipation of women "meant the emancipation of men, which allowed them to be rude to women." Shaw said, in substance, " 'If we are democrats, let us have votes for women; but if we are democrats, why on earth should we have respect for women?' "[2] At the same time, Shaw claimed in *Sixteen Self-Sketches* that not only was he always easily susceptible to women but that they pursued him eagerly from the time he was able to afford to dress well. Shaw was attracted to women's spontaneous expression of feeling and their serious participation in the roles of mother and mentor, while at the same time he was repelled by the frivolous, coquettish, "womanly-woman" roles which Victorian conventions assigned to women. Insofar as the "silly female" aspects of women were exhibited on the stage by scatterbrained actresses, he was vexed and irritated. A good part of his advice to Janet Achurch, Florence Farr, Ellen Terry, and Mrs. Campbell was aimed at curing them of stagey feminine wiles in order to cultivate their profounder abilities as actresses.

Most of the *Saturday Review* articles about actresses complain that the custom is to be theatrically, as opposed to naturally, beautiful, theatrical beauty requiring no brains. Pioneer unwomanly women, like Elizabeth Robins and Janet Achurch, never, Shaw laments, attain the popularity or recognition of those pretty and pleasant actresses who "enjoy a heyday of popular success by exhibiting themselves in expensive frocks, and going amiably through half a dozen tricks which they probably amuse themselves by teaching to their poodles when they are at a loss for something better to do" (II, 148).

In a review on May 2, 1896, Shaw discusses at great length the "brainless-susceptible" type in contrast to the "clever, positive" type. He observes that the brainless type is often lacking in beauty also, for her supposed beauty is not usually of the kind that would interest a sculptor or artist. The clever and intelligent type is hard to obtain for the stage, because women who are intelligent are able to make a living in professions other than acting, whereas women whose chief asset is "neurotic sexuality" gravitate automatically towards the stage. And since this kind of woman has "nothing but her sex to insist on, she insists on that continually" (II, 112-13).

A number of the letters in the correspondence which Shaw carried on with Florence Farr contain pointed advice. Florence Farr had a brief fling as an actress in some of Ibsen's plays and also, with Yeats as mentor, indulged a spooky art form which the two of them referred to as "cantillating." Shaw, counterpoising the occult inclinations of Yeats, told Florence Farr that she had "reached the stage of the Idiotically Beautiful. There remain the stages of the Intelligently Beautiful and finally of the Powerfully Beautiful."[3]

For Shaw, perfection in acting consisted of unremitting and exquisite sensuous appeal generated by profound reflection. He makes many pleas to actors and managers to establish standards of acting and often laments the lack of an academy in England, whose purpose it would be to set up curricula of training for actors. He complained that the old stock companies taught their actors stock gestures and stock expressions of stock emotions. But this mechanical method is no substitute for "a sense of beauty—the artistic sense—cultivated to such a degree of sensitiveness that a coarse or prosaic tone, or an awkward gesture, jars instantly on the artist as a note out of tune jars on the musician" (I, 211-12).

He also tells Florence Farr that if she is to be at all successful as Rebecca West in *Rosmersholm* she must have "a conception of [her] part so complete that it accounts for every moment of Rebecca's time whilst she is on the stage." This is a feat which Eleanora Duse, almost alone among actresses, was able to achieve, as we shall see presently. Even Janet Achurch, whom Shaw was able to praise, with reservations, at one time or another, was told that she replaced an interest in life and character with emotional stimulants "without the fatigue of thought" (III, 146).

Shaw was always campaigning for the reform of diction and deportment on the stage. "The very commonplaces of deportment are vanishing from the stage," he lamented (II, 191), nor are the actors aware that speech, gesture, and movement are the basis of acting as a fine art. They attempt to pass off affected diction upon their audience as the customary speech of aristocrats, whereas to the knowing members of the audience they sound more like the footmen and maids of lords and ladies than lords and ladies themselves (III, 107). There are a number of learned disquisitions on diction in the *Saturday Review* articles, in which Shaw mocks the pronunciation of vowels, of consonants, the location of accents—their dislocation, rather—and the queer pronunciations of common words. " 'Pawpialr' is charming: I would not for worlds have Miss Ashwell let it down into 'popular'; only I wish I could feel sure that she does it on purpose" (II, 40). When Shaw was engaged in making fun of Florence Farr's cantillations, he said that clear articulation and awareness of the meaning of one's words were more important than Yeats's fresh artificialities and impertinences.[4] Again, in the Preface to the Terry letters he brings up the subject of distinct articulation, asserting that slovenly speech is middle class, careful articulation aristocratic. And with customary candor he told Mrs. Campbell, "The first thing you have to knock into a stage novice is staccato alphabet so staccatissimo that every consonant will put out a candle at the back of the gallery. . . . I do not know who taught you to articulate; but whoever gave you your staccato gave you the power that, with your unaccountable fascination, enabled you, until you were found out, to persuade people that you were the supreme actress of your generation: no small feat for a woman who could not act at all except in fantasies of her own, like Irving."[5] In his letters to Golding Bright, Shaw advocated that a school of physical expression and rhetoric be added to London University, so that clergymen, lawyers, military officers—all people who speak in public— and especially actors would obtain conventional training in public speaking. "The first qualification I require from an actor is that he shall be able to impress

the back row of the gallery with his speech and bearing."[6] It was Forbes Robertson who received highest
praise from Shaw for the exquisite perfection of his
stage presence: "I wrote *Caesar and Cleopatra* for
Forbes Robertson, because he is the classic actor of our
day, and had a right to require such a service from me.
He stands completely aloof in simplicity, dignity, grace
and musical speech from the world of the motor car
and the Carlton Hotel, which so many others . . . prefer, or at least think they ought to pretend to prefer,
to the Olympian region where the classic actor is at
home."[7]

With the lack of an academy to set standards of
diction and modes of acting, Shaw had to fall back on
the director as the artistic co-ordinator and, indeed,
savior, of staged drama. And who might the best director of a play be but the author of the play himself,
especially if he was the author of *Arms and the Man*?

In his novel, *Love Among the Artists*, Shaw has a
good deal to say, via his Beethovenish Owen Jack,
about the art of acting and the shortcomings of actors.
Since this novel was written in 1881, we can see that
Shaw's views developed over a period of time and were
not invented for the sake of his articles in the *Saturday
Review*. When Magdalen Brailsford takes acting lessons from Owen Jack, she has a hard time. "She did
not enjoy her studies, for Jack was very exacting. . . .
The further she progressed, the less she could satisfy
him. His ear was far more acute than hers; and he demanded from her beauties of tone of which she had no
conception, and refinements of utterance which she
could not distinguish. He repeated sounds which he
declared were as distinct as day from night, and raged
at her because she could hear no difference between

them."[8] Shaw told Charles Charrington, the husband of Janet Achurch and himself an actor and all-around theater man: "I want a revival of the art of beautiful acting; and I know it to be impossible without tremendous practice and constant aiming at beauty of execution, not through a mechanical study of poses and pronunciations (though every actor should be a plastic and phonetic expert), but through a cultivation of delicate feeling, and absolute renunciation of all the coarser elements of popularity."[9] In a lecture he gave in 1889—"Acting, By One Who Does Not Believe in It"[10]—Shaw's thesis was that genuine acting, as opposed to artful shamming, consists of "metaphysical self-realization," by which he meant that the actor was not merely a gifted mimic but a well-defined self which could be realized through the roles he played. This meant that an actor could not legitimately play roles which did not express some element of his own personality. Instead of being a selfless potentiality that is realized through masks, the actor, according to Shaw, is a powerful self which becomes incarnated through appropriate roles. The view that acting is mere pretence and artifice is inadequate for Shaw, despite his insistence on beauty and grace of movement and diction. What distinguishes the great actor from the talented one is whether or not a powerful self is made real through the role he is playing.

We can see, also, from Martin Meisel's chapter on acting in *Shaw and the Nineteenth-Century Theater*, that Shaw's preference for a rhetorical and operatic style of acting is reconcilable with his notion of "metaphysical self-realization," since the powerful elements of personality can be suitably brought to light through a bold and musical style of acting, as opposed to an artificial and excessively delicate style like that of Henry Irving. This view obtains further support from Shaw's great fondness for Barry Sullivan (see below).

The arch vice of actors, however, was (as it still is) their inability to play any person other than themselves. Although at first glance this may seem inconsistent with the idea of "metaphysical self-realization," I think that what Shaw had in mind was a distinction between the actor's deepest self and his superficial manners and idiosyncrasies. When, in the reviews, he refers to actors playing themselves, he is virtually always speaking of their most superficial mannerisms. Either the play is adapted to these mannerisms by a compliant author, or the actors themselves adapt the play to suit their mannerisms. As Shaw observed in one of his reviews, "The title part was probably meant for Miss Ada Rehan rather than for Mrs John Wood; but Mrs John Wood can translate all sorts of parts into Mrs John Wood parts; so it does not greatly matter" (III, 151). As for Ada Rehan herself, "she has always practised the same adorable arts on me, by whatever name the playbill has called her" (III, 210).

This cultivation of the actor's overt and theatrical personality as a thing to be enjoyed for its own sake, independently of the play, can, of course, enable star actors to make gibberish seem wonderful by their charms,[11] a practice which Shaw blames on the emptiness of the mechanical well-made play. But if a demanding play calls upon them "to impersonate new characters instead of being presented with old characters that impersonate them—they lose their style, and even their ease and assurance" (II, 109). Shaw did not even think that the actors ought to save a bad play by overacting—for if the dramatist was not able to produce any subtlety of feeling, it was not up to the actor to rewrite the play for him. In fact, bad plays were the cause of the whole problem of the pre-eminence of the actor over the play. For as the young playgoer grew to adulthood and no longer found magical charm in stage productions and also, sad to say, found no great stimulation in the plays, he began to go to the theater to see the charms of the actors and actresses. Shaw found an inevitable solution to this degeneratory process: "In the long run nothing can retain the interest of the playgoer after the theatre has lost its illusion for his childhood, and its glamor for his adolescence, but a constant supply of interesting plays" (Essays, p. 137). He said that the younger actors who were in touch with the latest methods of performance were apt to be from outside the acting profession and free of the sentimental and hackneyed mannerisms which the children of old-time actors inherited. They were apt to be more intelligent and more literate too—and apt to perform Ibsen.

A good statement of the case of the actor versus the play occurs in a letter Shaw wrote to an Irish colleague in the 1920's:

As to stage technique, there are several stage techniques; and people may be very clever in one or more of them without being good at them all, and may even —especially in acting—know bits of them and not the rest. The beginning and end of the business from the author's point of view is the art of making the audience believe that real things are happening to real people. But the actor, male or female, may want the audience to believe that it is witnessing a magnificent display of acting by a great artist; and when the attempt to do this fails, the effect is disastrous, because then there is neither play nor great acting: the play is not credible nor the acting fascinating. To your star actor the play does not exist except as a mounting block. That is why comparatively humble actors, who do not dare to think they can succeed apart from the play, often give much better representations than star casts.[12]

So many of the reviews in the *Saturday Review* denounced the obtruding actor—whether Irving, Bernhardt, or Mrs. Campbell—that when Shaw finally saw a play in which the actors produced a semblance of real people other than themselves he wrote: "And yet it produced what very few plays at the St James's produce: that is, a strong illusion that we were looking at the persons and events of Mr Potter's story, and not merely at our friends Mr Alexander, Miss Neilson, and party, in their newest summer costumes. At the end of the first act, a gentleman in the audience so completely forgot Mr Alexander's identity, that he got up and indignantly remonstrated with him for the blackguardism with which he was behaving in the character of 'the Babe' " (III, 365).

Shaw's discussions of the direction of plays have the distinction of combining high, almost relentless, artistic standards with affection and charity for the actor and the director. The consistency of his statements on the subject is quite remarkable when one observes that more than fifty years separate the first and last passages on play-directing quoted below.

After an unsatisfactory performance in October, 1895, Shaw wrote: "The artistic manager, as distinguished from the man who merely takes a theatre and puts up a play, is also a critic, and, knowing the difference between finished stage execution and mere larking, picks and drills his company accordingly. That is how theatres come to have styles as well as individuals"

(I, 214). From a letter already quoted[13] and from the "Rules for Directors"[14] we obtain a full picture of the obligations of the director. He must have the performance thoroughly worked out before he or the actors appear at rehearsal. Every minute detail of movement and inflection must be clearly in his mind, for if it is not the actors will lose confidence in his ability and feel that the entire process of staging the play is arbitrary and whimsical. The ideal director is the author of the play, who should select the cast without caring whether they understand the play or not. And, says the author of "Don Juan in Hell," the principal actors should be soprano, alto, tenor, and bass. The author should read the play to the cast and then have the players go through it with their books in hand. Later, when the actors have memorized the play, the director should take a seat in the orchestra and let the play be acted through, all the time making notes but never interrupting the actors, "no matter how completely the play goes to pieces, as it must at first when the players are trying to remember their parts and cues so desperately that they are incapable of acting."[15] Not until the play is mechanically perfect and entirely memorized should the director interrupt the acting.

Shaw's consideration for the actors is touching and impressive. Outsiders should not be allowed at rehearsals, but if for some reason an outsider is present, the actor must never be reproved, never corrected. And during private rehearsals:

> Never find fault until you know the remedy; and never discuss a passage with a player; shew how the passage should be done as a suggestion, not an order; and exaggerate your demonstration sufficiently to prevent the player giving a mere imitation of it.[16]

In arranging hours players with only a few lines to speak should not be kept hanging about all day whilst the principals are rehearsing. Late night rehearsals are most objectionable. Neither players nor directors should work when they ought to be in bed. If such rehearsals are unavoidable the players who are kept too late for their last trains or buses should be paid their taxi fares home.[17]

When a player repeatedly omits some physical feat or movement, the director must conclude that it is made impossible by some infirmity which the player would rather die than disclose. In such cases the business must be altered.[18]

Of the many actors whom Shaw discusses in the dramatic reviews of the nineties, Mrs. Campbell and Henry Irving receive the most attention. But there are many important remarks to and about Ellen Terry, Richard Mansfield, and Janet Achurch in Shaw's letters. And although Eleonora Duse did not perform very many times between 1895 and 1898 in Shaw's presence, she appears over and over again in the reviews as a paragon of acting, especially in contrast to Sarah Bernhardt.

Some mention ought to be made of the famous Ellen Terry, and yet there is not very much to be said which the correspondence does not deal with sufficiently. Ellen Terry appears infrequently in the *Saturday Review* articles and always to the accompaniment of the same tune. When she played in *King Arthur* in 1895 Shaw wrote:

As to Miss Ellen Terry, it was the old story, a born actress of real women's parts condemned to figure as a mere artist's model in costume plays which, from the woman's point of view, are foolish flatteries written by gentlemen for gentlemen. It is pathetic to see Miss Terry snatching at some fleeting touch of nature in her part, and playing it not only to perfection, but often with a parting caress that brings it beyond that for an instant as she relinquishes it, very loth, and passes on to the next length of arid sham-feminine twaddle in blank verse, which she pumps out in little rhythmic strokes in a desperate and all too obvious effort to make music of it. (I, 17)

Little need be added to this, for in this review as in almost every other review involving Ellen Terry or Henry Irving, Shaw laments Ellen Terry's indissoluble attachment to the Lyceum, her willingness to remain faithful to Irving, and her reluctance to give up pretty-as-a-picture touches of nature for the role of the new woman, for Ibsen.

A recurring childhood idol throughout the three volumes of dramatic criticism is Barry Sullivan. He was a touring actor in Shaw's youth who evidently managed to dazzle the boy with the rhetorical brilliance of his acting. A fine physical specimen with a grand presence, Sullivan was "the very incarnation of the old individualistic, tyrannical conception of a great actor" (I, 271). Although, as Shaw claims, a number of critics saw Irving as the inheritor of the Sullivan style, Shaw points out that Irving, after a brief but absurd period as thunderer, reacted against the Sullivan manner and cultivated a delicate and refined stage style, the very opposite of the early nineteenth-century school.

Shaw has particular praise for Sullivan's Shakespeare, for while the English stage, as represented by the London West End, trifled with Cup and Saucer drama and the well-made play, Sullivan toured the

provinces with his great success, *Hamlet*. This "prince-
ly stroller"[19] was not a mere swaggerer, however: "He
had classic taste and noble judgment for older critics
too. In Hamlet's scene with Ophelia he never senti-
mentalized it to drag in vulgar sex appeal as Irving did.
As to treating the closet scene as an example of the
Oedipus complex, such notions did not exist for him.
His natural force was so great that he had not to stoke
himself with drink as Kean, Robson, and even Dickens
in America killed themselves prematurely by doing."[20]
Indeed, Sullivan's great success, for Shaw, was his ability to inspire the young. "When I was a very im-
pressionable boy he became my model of personal
nobility."[21]

About Sarah Bernhardt Shaw had little to say that
was favorable. "As to Madame Bernhardt's own performance, it is not humanly possible for an actress to
do very much with a play in which, when the other
characters are not describing what a peerlessly beautiful
and wonderful creature she is, she is herself on the
stage accepting that ridiculous position" (I, 159).
Shaw does note that she has managed to decrease the
quantity of her make-up—she had a face instead of a
stucco mask—a correction which possibly indicates that
Bernhardt had read Shaw's satirical review of her on
June 15, 1895. But her acting, to use Shaw's phrase, remained pure rant. Her method was to tear through
her lines, seemingly unaware of what she was saying,
with her frenzy becoming more intense as the play
progressed. The audience, unfortunately, unable to
distinguish between the hollow force of rant and real
acting, irritated Shaw by cheering Bernhardt vigorously. Instead of acting, Shaw protested, she offered
the audience odds and ends from her old successes:

reputation instead of acting. As for her monotone, Shaw advised her "to add a complete set of strings to her lyre" (I, 162). Shaw's descriptions of her are always of a woman trying to create a sensation. The "vulgar and commercial" performances of Bernhardt were bad enough, but when these performances were in "claptraps" constructed by Sardou, Shaw found the "whole affair . . . antiquated and ridiculous, except when I regard it as a high modern development of the circus and the waxworks" (I, 138). Two years later, Shaw summed her up once again, her qualities already having been crystallized into a Shavian "character" which was to remain pretty much the same whenever a reference to Bernhardt was needed again:

Every year Madame Bernhardt comes to us with a new play, in which she kills somebody with any weapon from a hairpin to a hatchet; intones a great deal of dialogue as a sample of what is called "the golden voice," . . . goes through her well-known feat of tearing a passion to tatters at the end of the second or fourth act, according to the length of the piece; serves out a certain ration of the celebrated smile; and between whiles gets through any ordinary acting that may be necessary in a thoroughly businesslike and competent fashion. This routine constitutes a permanent exhibition, which is refurnished every year with fresh scenery, fresh dialogue, and a fresh author, whilst remaining itself invariable. (III, 175)

As consistently as Shaw finds fault with Bernhardt, so consistently does he praise Eleonora Duse. He even goes so far as to devote a whole review to an examination of their claims as actresses (June 15, 1895). Duse, of course, wins without a contest. She has a qualification almost unknown to actors—her "every part is a separate creation," whereas Bernhardt "does not enter into the leading character: she substitutes herself for it." When Duse comes onstage, "you are quite welcome to take your opera-glass and count whatever lines time and care have so far traced on her. They are the credentials of her humanity; and she knows better than to obliterate that significant handwriting beneath a layer of peachbloom from the chemist's. The shadows on her face are grey, not crimson; her lips are sometimes nearly grey also; there are neither dabs nor dimples; her charm could never be imitated by a barmaid with unlimited pin money and a row of footlights before her" (I, 150). The distinction which Shaw makes between Duse's real face, reflecting as it does her inner nature, and the false face which other actors obtain by means of cosmetics, reinforces his distinction between the actor's "metaphysical self-realization" and mere display of mannerisms. According to the review of June 8, 1895, Duse's performances represented the best modern acting that Shaw had ever seen. His description of the particular strength of her acting is one of the most definitive treatments of acting as a fine art to be found in his writing:

The majority of actresses never get beyond learning not to invent new points for themselves, but rather to pick out in their parts the passages which admit of certain well worn and tried old points being reapplied. When they have learned to make these points smoothly and to keep quiet between whiles with a graceful air of having good reasons for doing nothing, they are finished actresses. The great actress has a harder struggle. She goes on inventing her points and her business determinedly, constantly increasing the original half-dozen, and constantly executing them with greater force and smoothness. A time comes when she is always making points, and making them well; and this is the finishing point with some actresses. But with the greatest artists there soon commences an integration of the points into a continuous whole, at which stage the actress appears to make no points at all, and to proceed in the most unstudied and "natural" way. This rare consummation Duse has reached. . . . There are years of work, bodily and mental, behind every instant of it—work, mind, not mere practice and habit, which is quite a different thing. It is the rarity of gigantic energy needed to sustain this work which makes Duse so exceptional; for the work is in her case highly intellectual work, and so requires energy of a quality altogether superior to the mere head of steam needed to produce Bern-hardtian explosions with the requisite regularity. (I, 146-47)

Shaw's relationship with Richard Mansfield, who was both an actor and producer in the United States and who had a great success with *Arms and the Man*, clarifies some of the problems which Shaw had to cope with as a critic and as a dramatist seeking satisfactory actors. During the period when he was writing for the *Saturday Review* he was also trying to get *Candida* staged in England and America. Mansfield had signed a contract to produce *Candida* with Janet Achurch, and a correspondence between him and Shaw ensued in which Shaw gave him strong advice, bordering on commands. Shaw obviously did not trust Mansfield's instincts and felt it was necessary to urge him to re-strain himself, in order to avoid giving an inaccurately balanced representation of *Candida*. He wrote Janet Achurch that Mansfield's repertory consisted of "one-man entertainments requiring only the 'character acting' which is now falling into disrepute in England as mere entertainer's work."[22] Shortly before *Candida* was to have its premiere, Mansfield backed down and refused to produce it. He wrote Shaw an astonishingly harebrained letter, complaining about the hyper-intellectuality of the play and remarking, "You'll have to write a play that a man can play and about a woman that heroes fought for and a bit of ribbon that a knight tied to his lance. The stage is for romance and love and truth and honor."[23] What Mansfield admired was the stagey exhibitionism that Shaw despised, a fact that Shaw perceived early enough to have told Mansfield, "There are no points: the entire work is one sustained point from beginning to end."[24] But Mansfield's limitations were similar to those which Shaw experienced regularly in the producers of the plays he was then reviewing, except that in this case Shaw was the victim.

Shaw's relationship with Mrs. Patrick Campbell extended from the early nineties until 1941. Stella Campbell's sudden success was made possible by *The Second Mrs. Tanqueray*, a play which Shaw already regarded as old-fashioned when it was revived in 1895, the year in which he began his criticisms of plays for the *Saturday Review*. His first extensive treatment of Mrs. Campbell appeared in March, 1895, when she had the lead in Pinero's next success, *The Notorious Mrs. Ebbsmith*. Because the play was so bad, said Shaw, it set Mrs. Campbell free to do as she pleased, "the result being an irresistible projection of that lady's personal genius" (I, 61). The word "personal" is the key word, for at the start of this drama between Stella and Joey (as she came to address Shaw in later years) Shaw allowed himself to be given over to rapture upon rapture. Stella's personal genius, of course, was her person: "She creates all sorts of illusions, and gives one all sorts of searching sensations. It is impossible not to feel that those haunting eyes are brooding on a momentous past, and the parted lips anticipating a thrilling imminent future, whilst some enigmatic present must no less surely be working underneath all that subtle play of limb and stealthy intensity of tone. . . . When the curtain comes down, you are compelled to admit that, after all, nothing has come of it except your conviction that Mrs Patrick Campbell is a wonderful woman" (I, 61). This marks the beginning of the rhapsodies in print. When Mrs. Campbell appears in Sardou's *Fedora* in May, 1895, we are taken yet a bit further into the critic's confidence: "The moment she was seen, our reason collapsed and our judgment fled. Every time the curtain fell there was a delirious roar. If the play was not tragic, our infatuation was. I solemnly warn all and sundry that no common man's opinion of the artistic merits of that performance was worth a farthing after the first flash of the heroine's eyes. It was not Fedora; but it was Circe; and I, as sworn critic, must make the best attempt I can to be Ulysses" (I, 134-35). But quite early in his rhapsodies over Mrs. Campbell, we find that Shaw is not particularly pleased with her ability as an actress. The disillusion begins moderately enough, but the process is rapid. The initial limitation of Mrs. Campbell's acting is her lack of variety. Although she can be forceful, her force has "only one mode, and that one the vituperative." As a result, the only intensity she shows is the intensity of rage. This is charitably summed up in Shaw's conclusion that Mrs. Campbell "is not yet mistress of her art," although she has a number of qualifications. Unfortunately, her diction is not one of them.

Shaw very magnanimously says that he will forgive her saying "forgimme" for "forgive me," but "hatrid" and "disseived" he finds odious (I, 135-36).

Finally, although Mrs. Campbell was capable of displaying Sarah Bernhardt's histrionics, she could not manage to play Fedora, only Mrs. Patrick Campbell. "It was irrelevant; but it was effective" (I, 136).

Shaw is now and then able to give Mrs. Campbell some small praise—she was a better Mrs. Ebbsmith than Olga Nethersole, she has great dexterity and is able to maneuver quite naturally with her hands while she is speaking her speeches, and as Juliet in Shakespeare "she danced like the daughter of Herodias" (I, 127, 202). But her acting tends to be inept: "As Juliet she still fits herself into the hospitable manly heart without effort, simply because she is a wonderful person, not only in mere facial prettiness ... but in the extraordinary swiftness and certainty of her physical self-command. ... Her Juliet, nevertheless, is an immature performance at all the exceptional points which, please remember, are not very numerous, much of Juliet's business being of a kind that no 'leading lady' of ordinary ability could possibly fail in. ... Nothing of it is memorable except the dance—the irresistible dance" (I, 202-03). The alternation of praise and blame here is strange indeed, but despite the vertigo which seems to have inspired it, Shaw is still able to see black as black.

When Mrs. Campbell returned to the London stage in February, 1896, to play in *For the Crown,* Shaw resumed making statements simultaneously extravagant and sober. Perhaps Mrs. Campbell had improved a bit since her previous appearance, for she managed some tenderness and mellowed her diction, and even restrained her tendency toward vituperation. But the question remained: Could she act? "Who said she could?—who wants her to act?—who cares two-pence whether she possesses that or any other second-rate accomplishment? On the highest plane one does not act, one *is*. Go and see her move, stand, speak, look, kneel—go and breathe the magic atmosphere that is created by the grace of all these deeds; and then talk to me about acting, forsooth!" (II, 65). After this, the criticism gets more harsh and violent. When Mrs. Campbell played in *Magda*, an adaptation of Suder-mann's *Home*, in June, 1896, she inspired Shaw to observe that when great masterpieces like *Magda* are played for the public, great actors should be hired to perform them. Mrs. Campbell's acting was "merest baby-play" (II, 148) compared with the acting of Elizabeth Robins or Janet Achurch. Shaw attributed the failure of the play entirely to Mrs. Campbell. Only her grace of bearing prevented her from looking as silly as she actually was, and when one of the great emotional crises of the play arrived, "Mrs Campbell did not display as much feeling as an ordinary woman of fifty does at the arrival of the postman. Whether her non-entity at this point was the paralysis of a novice who does not know how to express what she feels, or whether it was the vacuity of a woman who does not feel at all, I cannot determine" (II, 146-47). In her favor, all Shaw can observe is that if she is not a great actress, at least she is a great artist (II, 149). Probably no one else inspired in Shaw a more enigmatic utterance.

The climax of invective against Mrs. Campbell's acting, or non-acting, occurs in a brilliant review of Ibsen's *Little Eyolf*, entitled "Ibsen Without Tears," which, as any Shavian knows, is not the way Ibsen should be performed. Ironic contrast is made throughout between Janet Achurch's performance of Rita Allmers and Mrs. Campbell's. Mrs. Campbell's unspoken refrain throughout the performance was " 'You silly people: what are you making all this fuss about?' " (II, 272). "And how nicely Mrs Campbell took the drowning of the child! Just a pretty waving of the fingers, a moderate scream as if she had very nearly walked on a tin tack, and it was all over, without tears, without pain, without more fuss than if she had broken the glass of her watch" (II, 273). The final catastrophe was somewhat dreadful and Shaw merciless, for "in the third act, the smoothness of the proceedings was somewhat marred by the fact that Mrs Campbell, not knowing her words, had to stop acting and frankly bring the book on the stage and read from it" (II, 274).

After this, there is nothing of much consequence concerning Mrs. Campbell in *Our Theatres in the Nineties*. She "even acts occasionally" (III, 53) in one play and puts in a decent performance of Ophelia in *Hamlet* (III, 205).

By 1914 Shaw could look back on Mrs. Campbell's career with a more comprehensive view, as he does in a letter to George C. Tyler, October 12, 1914, dealing with a production of *Pygmalion* in New York:

It is no use arguing; she is clever enough to talk your hair gray; but she has no more judgment than a baby, and will spoil the play if you will let her. She does not know where the interest of the play really comes; and does not care twopence about the part, to which she has never given five minutes' serious thought, except as an excuse for fascinating and a joke. . . . She can give a charming performance if she likes and if she sticks loyally to the text and does not gag or play for silly laughs. . . . The moral of all this is that for her sake and for your own you must stick to me and to the play, and resist all her wiles to have it cut down . . . if mortal man can resist such a siren, which I rather doubt.[25]

As far as the reviews indicate, Shaw had great admiration for Janet Achurch. She was a pioneer performer of Ibsen, playing the role of Nora in the first English performance of *A Doll's House*, and her husband, Charles Charrington, who produced this performance, later took it to Australia, where his wife continued to play Nora. But from Shaw's letters, we learn that Janet Achurch was going downhill during the very years Shaw wrote for the *Saturday Review*, although there is little evidence of his growing dissatisfaction in the reviews themselves, because the Charringtons were not often in London while he was reviewing.

Shaw met Janet Achurch on June 16, 1889, at a dinner given to celebrate the production of *A Doll's House*.[26] He found her interesting right away and his subsequent letters to her are simultaneously serious and flirty in the manner we have become accustomed to in most of his letters to women. After the dinner, he wrote to her to describe how magnetized he was by her stage personality. But in 1892, after she had played Nora for several years, Shaw wrote her a very critical letter about the coarsening of her performance. Speaking to her in the third person, to soften his blows, he says, ". . . but she has scandalously neglected to cultivate the beautiful, reposeful, quietly expressive, infinitely inflectionable normal voice, neither raised nor lowered, which is the great charm of a fine speaker."[27] He is critical of many details of gesture and voice, but concludes that her comprehension of Nora is extraordinary. By 1895, however, things begin to deteriorate. Janet Achurch is gradually addicted to morphine and alcohol to allay her depressions and her acting begins to take on Bernhardtian superficiality. At first Shaw is gentle and tells her that she is too good for trashy plays, Pinero and light comedy especially, and that she should save her showy histrionics until her declining years.[28] He even tries to persuade her to play Julia in his own *The Philanderer*. But by the time she arrives in New York to play *Candida* with Richard Mansfield, the *Candida* that never materialized, Shaw felt it imperative to give her some harsh warnings:

Observe, Janet Achurch, what you have to do is to play the part. You have not to make a success. New York must notice nothing: it must say "Of course," and go home quietly. If it says "Hooray" then you will be a mere popular actress, a sort of person whom I utterly decline to know. You must confine yourself strictly to your business, and do that punctually and faithfully, undisturbed by any covetings of success for yourself or me or the play. It does not matter whether the play fails or not, or whether you are admired or not; it is sufficient if you gain the respect of the public and your fellow artists, which you cannot fail to do if only you will keep yourself to the point.[29]

In a very important and brilliant letter of March 23, 1895, Shaw lectures Janet Achurch on her drug addiction, her exhibitionism as an actress, and her lack of "religion." He describes his good influence upon her and encourages her to allow it to grow: "Janet at last wakes to the emotion under which I have abstained; and for a while she rapidly begins to draw on rich stores of life, becomes beautiful, becomes real, becomes almost saintly, looks at me with eyes that have no glamor of morphia in them, and with an affection that is not hysterical, though in the middle of it all she stabs me to the heart by dyeing her hair a refulgent yellow. The question is, how am I to make Janet religious, so that she may recreate herself and feel no need of stimulants. That is the question that obsesses me."[30] Her concern for success, her independence and unreliability, her aversion to adhering to contracts, her squandering of her friends' money on the production of plays that failed—all of these distressed Shaw and caused him to lecture her over and over again. The letters become almost too depressing to read as one sees the way her dramatic gifts are gradually destroyed by her psychological problems, about which Shaw can do nothing. Pathetically he writes her: "It is clear that you are not going to act any more: it is all Sarah Bernhardt now—no brains, no pains, none of the distinction and freshness of thoughtful, self controlled work, nothing but letting yourself go and giving it to 'em hot and strong now that you have found that they will stand it."[31] These letters, of which I have supplied only a distillation, provide a short course in Shaw's theory of acting.

Shaw's quarrel with Irving, which began in the 1895 reviews of Lyceum productions and never actually came to an end before Shaw's death, provides a number of the idées fixes which run through Shaw's criticism. As an actor-manager, Irving was in a position to exploit his own abilities as an actor while paying a minimum of attention to the qualities and the types of drama he produced at the Lyceum—the main qualification of a play being, of course, that it contained a part suited to the talents of the actor-manager. Indeed, the history of the Lyceum during Irving's reign bears out Shaw's objections to the actor-manager system in general and to Irving in particular, for both acting talent and playwriting talent were lavishly wasted. Although much of Shaw's *Saturday Review* criticism resulted in practical improvements, he was never able to produce any change in the practices of Irving.

While most of his references to Irving consist of fulminations against his stupidity and egomania, Shaw did not fail to give him his due. Despite everything, Irving managed to make a substantial contribution to the art of acting, a contribution which Shaw claimed he had been able to detect early in Irving's career. Speaking of the touring companies of actors which he had seen in Dublin in his youth, Shaw wrote in the Preface to the Terry letters:

Among these London successes which brought London productions unchanged to Dublin was a play called The Two Roses, by Albery. One of the characters was a selfish old humbug named Digby Grant. It made the success of the piece by a certain egotistical intensity, sinister and yet dignified in its indignity, which was not in the play but in the actor: an actor with a tall thin figure, which, if it could not be convicted of grotesqueness was certainly indescribably peculiar, and a voice which was dependent so much on the resonance of a cavernous nose that it was, compared to the powerful and musical chest voice of Barry Sullivan, a highly cultivated neigh. His name was Henry Irving. I instinctively felt that a new drama inhered in this man, though I then had no conscious notion that I was destined to write it.[32]

Even with his bad voice, however, Irving had qualities that could not be underestimated. To begin with, he had a passion for acting—he was, as Shaw put it, stagestruck.[33] "He could give importance and a noble melancholy to any sort of drivel that was put into his mouth."[34] He had cultivation; he had refinement. In fact, Shaw points out that in his performance as the Vicar of Wakefield, Irving had so much cultivation that he ruined the part (III, 38). Shaw is able to refer to Irving more than once as England's greatest representative of acting as a fine art. After the school of Edmund Kean and the thunderers, it was Irving's great achievement "to re-establish on the stage the touching, appealing nobility of sentiment and affection" (I, 273). Irving was able to bring an unfamiliar delicacy to the stage after a long period of rhetorical bombast and flamboyance. Not surprisingly, then, Irving eventually reached a position of eminence and distinction which made it not unseemly for him to request that acting be put among the fine arts by being officially recognized by the state. In a famous article in the *Saturday Review*, February 9, 1895, Shaw describes Irving's public lecture requesting "official recognition" of actors as artists. He then goes on to expound its indirections by observing: " 'The artist who composed the music for King Arthur is Sir Arthur Sullivan; the artist who composed the poem which made King Arthur known to this generation died Lord Tennyson; the artist who designed the suit of armor worn by King Arthur is Sir Edward Burne-Jones: why should the artist who plays King Arthur be only Mister Henry Irving?' " (I, 32) Indeed, Shaw is entirely on his side, for he believed that in advancing a claim to knighthood Irving had done worthily and courageously: "worthily, because a title can add nothing to his personal eminence, and courageously, because many unworthy persons will wound him by seeing nothing in the act but a vain man grasping at a handle for his name" (I, 33). But after this admirably disinterested vindication of Irving's opinion of the art of acting, Shaw gives the first blow in a battle that continued long after Irving's death in 1905. After quoting several indifferent remarks which Irving made about Wagner and Mendelssohn, remarks, however, couched in rather vapid poetic prose, Shaw observes that "this quotation, by the way, also proves that Mr Irving does not know fine literature from penny-a-liner's fustian" (I, 34). Ironically enough, as Shaw well knew, Irving did not write his own speeches.

Shaw's objections to Irving were that he worshiped himself above all; that he mutilated the dramas he produced, especially Shakespearean drama; that he was ignorant and without taste; that he prevented other actors from realizing their own abilities because of his tyranny over them; and that he did nothing to further the drama of his own time. Irving's years in control of the Lyceum resulted in "the steady cultivation of the actor as a personal force" and the Lyceum's neglect of the drama (III, 39). Audiences crowded to the Lyceum to see Henry Irving, not to see Shakespeare or, had Irving performed him, Ibsen. The result of this star system, as historians of the drama and modern play anthologies clearly indicate, was a dearth of worthwhile plays. Furthermore, as long as the actor was the *raison d'être* of the theater, even the plays that did appear on the stage appeared in a somewhat mutilated form. For while it was the aim of the actor to display himself, the play did not matter as a work of art but merely as a vehicle.

When Irving played Richard III, his performance not only contradicted the meaning of the lines but their spirit and feeling. "This, however, we are used to: Sir Henry Irving never did and never will make use of a play otherwise than as a vehicle for some fantastic creation of his own" (II, 291). On another occasion, a review of Augustin's Filon's book *The English Stage*, Shaw is able to quote Filon's similar estimation of Irving's dramatic method. Filon writes: "Irving was not only able to impart more meaning to his words than they expressed in themselves, but was addicted even to making them subservient to his own ideas, and making the public accept his conception in face of a text which was in flat contradiction to it." Shaw is unable to resist adding: "If M. Filon had said not only that Sir Henry Irving is able to do this, but that he is not able to do anything else; that he is the despair of all authors and true Shakespeareans in consequence; that he has practically abolished interpretation on the Lyceum stage and substituted the acting of his own fancies for it . . . he would have said nothing that is not latent in his observation about the power to act in flat contradiction to the text—or what is left of the text—in the Lyceum 'acting editions'" (III, 154-55). And in a Drydenesque vein: "Sir Henry Irving is completely independent of the dramatist, and only approaches him in moments of aberration" (III, 185). "His Hamlet and his Lear were to many people more interesting than Shakespear's Hamlet and Lear; but the two pairs were hardly even related" (*Pen Portraits*, p. 266).

In a rather dubious compliment, Shaw observes that sometimes Irving's creations were a real improvement over the original, most particularly his version of Iachimo in his production of *Cymbeline* (II, 292). Probably the most famous characterization of Irving's treatment of a play is to be found in the review of *Cymbeline* on September 26, 1896. After discussing

Irving's curious lack of taste and judgment, a deficiency which makes it easy for him to omit the best passages of the play, Shaw examines Irving's other shortcomings:

This curious want of connoisseurship in literature would disable Sir Henry Irving seriously if he were an interpretative actor. But it is, happily, the fault of a great quality—the creative quality. A prodigious deal of nonsense has been written about Sir Henry Irving's conception of this, that, and the other Shakespearean character. The truth is that he has never in his life conceived or interpreted the characters of any author except himself. He is really as incapable of acting another man's play as Wagner was of setting another man's libretto; and he should, like Wagner, have written his plays for himself. But as he did not find himself out until it was too late for him to learn that supplementary trade, he was compelled to use other men's plays as the framework for his own creations. His first great success in this sort of adaptation was with the Merchant of Venice. There was no question then of a bad Shylock or a good Shylock: he was simply not Shylock at all; and when his own creation came into conflict with Shakespear's, as it did quite openly in the Trial scene, he simply played in flat contradiction of the lines, and positively acted Shakespear off the stage. (II, 198)

The review goes on to point out that whereas these new creations do not work when the actor must compete with Shakespeare, they can be quite successful in the case of inferior plays having little character of their own. The Irving treatment of Shakespeare had by 1897 so far become the Lyceum norm that when Forbes Robertson appeared in a production of Hamlet, also at the Lyceum but without the services of Irving, Shaw noted that there were passages in the play in which the audience's attention was actually taken off the starring actor and, even more remarkable, that the story of the play was perfectly intelligible. "What is the Lyceum coming to?" he asked. "Is it for this that Sir Henry Irving has invented a whole series of original romantic dramas, and given the credit of them without a murmur to the immortal bard . . . ?" (III, 200) In later years, when he wrote the preface to his correspondence with Ellen Terry, Shaw looked back on Irving's Hamlet to observe that it "was neither skilled classic acting nor Shakespear's Hamlet" and that "compared to Sullivan he was a limp duffer and compared to Robertson a freak."[35]

The shreds and patches which Irving and his predecessors tore out of his [Shakespeare's] plays and tacked crudely together for performances which were interrupted four or five times by intolerable intervals, during which the women in the audience sat in silent boredom whilst the men wandered about the corridors and refreshment bars, were endurable only by people who, knowing no better, thought they were assisting at a very firstrate solemnization, and were helped by that illusion to persuade themselves that they were enjoying the best that a great institution and two great performers [Irving and Ellen Terry] could do for them. I knew better.[36]

Shaw attributed Irving's shortcomings to an excess of imagination and self-adoration allied with a deficiency of intelligence and taste, a combination which one would more or less expect to result in the kind of actor Irving proved to be—rhetorical, picturesque, poetic. But these qualities, though essential to refined theater, will not suffice for a dramatic repertory as well as they do for the repertory of a ballet company. To an intellectual like Shaw, exquisite representations of emotional states are admirable, provided they are not at the expense of matter for thought.

Irving's lack of intellectuality furnished a constant butt for Shavian wit. After a dramatic version of scenes from *Don Quixote*, Irving came before the curtain to make a little speech: "When he came before the curtain at the end, he informed us, with transparent good faith, that the little play practically covered the whole of Cervantes' novel, a statement which we listened to with respectful stupefaction. I get into trouble often enough by my ignorance of authors whom every literate person is expected to have at his fingers' ends; but I believe Mr Irving can beat me hollow in that respect. If I have not read Don Quixote all through, I have at least looked at the pictures; and I am prepared to swear that Mr Irving never got beyond the second chapter" (I, 115). After Irving's death in 1905, Shaw began to speak even more candidly, although there is a letter to Ellen Terry, dated October 2, 1896, reporting Shaw's impression of Irving during one of the rare personal encounters between them: "I liked Henry, though he is without exception absolutely the stupidest man I ever met. Simply no brains—nothing but character and temperament. Curious, how little mere brains are!" When Irving died, Shaw wrote to Ellen Terry: "Laurence, who is coming to lunch with me on Wednesday, says the family regard me as a most unmitigated Yahoo, and assures me, very Irvingesquely, that his father was so truly kindhearted that he would willingly have paid my funeral expenses at any time. Such is the unquenchable heart of youth."[37]

Shaw never forgave Irving for wasting the talents of Ellen Terry in his picturesque desecrations of Shakespeare, especially since she was faithful to Irving to the last. There is an extraordinary number of letters in the Shaw—Terry volume which deal with Ellen Terry's reluctance to start off on her own career, independent of Irving, and to play Lady Cicely in *Captain Brassbound's Conversion*, a role written especially for her. Furthermore, Shaw felt that in failing to do modern plays, particularly those of Ibsen, Irving was not only preventing Ellen Terry from developing her capabilities as an actress but also doing a great disservice to the cause of modern drama:

The Lyceum is incorrigible: its debt to modern dramatic art is now too far in arrear ever to be paid. After all, why, after inventing a distinct *genre* of art, and an undeniably fascinating one at that, should Sir Henry Irving now place himself at the disposition of Ibsen, and become the Exponent of Another on the stage which he has hitherto trodden as the Self-Expounded? Why should Miss Terry, whom we have adored under all sorts of delicious, nonsensical disguises, loving especially those which made her most herself, turn mere actress, and be transformed by Norwegian enchantments into an embodiment of those inmost reproaches of conscience which we now go to the Lyceum to forget? (III, 31-32)

A few weeks after this, Shaw laments that Ellen Terry must extract a precarious existence from playing in Shakespeare and laments, "What an artist we have thrown to our national theatrical Minotaur. . . . my regard for Sir Henry Irving cannot blind me to the fact that it would have been better for us twenty-five years ago to have tied him up in a sack with every existing copy of the works of Shakespear, and dropped him into the crater of the nearest volcano" (III, 37-38).

The most thoroughgoing denunciation of the Lyceum policy occurs in the review of July 17, 1897: the Lyceum produces old-fashioned and outdated drama; Ellen Terry is treated as a beautiful living picture; modern audiences of the first rank want "realistic drama of complete brainy, passional texture all through, and will not have any pictorial stuff or roulade at all"; the old-fashioned play with its blustery rhetoric, sentimentality, and pictorial decorations is out of date; the simple-minded pretty-as-a-picture use of leading ladies, popularized by Irving's use of Ellen Terry, will not impose any longer in "more critical quarters" (III, 194-95).

Also in 1897, Irving misunderstood Shaw's review of his performance of *Richard III*, in which Shaw described him as lacking control. Irving believed that Shaw was accusing him of drunkenness, which was not the case, and he sent Shaw an angry letter. Shaw replied that the idea that Irving might have been drunk had never entered his mind: "I am sorry that the article should have caused you any uneasiness; but my vanity as a critic is severely wounded by your very cheap estimate of the sort of work I do. If you knew the trouble your performances give me—you are in some ways the most difficult subject a critic can tackle, and quite the most exasperating for an author-critic—you would be astonished at my patience and amiability."[38] And he assures Irving that if he believed him drunk, he would have said so directly or said nothing. Irving wrote a nasty reply: "You are absolutely wrong in your polite insinuation of the cat out of the bag—as I had not the privilege of reading your criticism—as you call it—of Richard. I never read a criticism of yours in my life. I have read lots of your droll, amusing, irrelevant and sometimes impertinent pages, but criticism containing judgment and sympathy I have never seen by your pen."[39]

His best and most dramatic treatment of Irving is to be found in an article on Irving's death, written in October, 1905, and published in a distorted translation, in the *Neue Freie Presse* of Vienna. Its honest but bleak intensity brought severe censure upon Shaw and seemed to vindicate the not uncommon picture of him as a callous ogre. When Shaw pointed out to the London papers that they had retranslated back into English what was originally a defective translation itself, he received little heed, despite his placing at their disposal the original and uncorrupted text.

Although it is a desecration to chop the piece into bits, a few key passages are indispensable:

When I was asked, the day after his death, to pay a tribute to his memory, I wrote: "He did nothing for the living drama; and he mutilated the remains of the dying Shakespear; but he won his lifelong fight to have the actor recognized as the peer of all other artists; and this was enough for one man to accomplish. *Requiescat in pace.*" The truth is that Irving took no interest in anything except himself; and he was not interested even in himself except as an imaginary figure in an imaginary setting. . . . His Mathias in The Bells and his Charles I were elaborated to the most extreme degree. They were such miracles of finished execution that they raised a melodrama of no importance and a surpassingly bad historical play into dramatic masterpieces. . . . In judging Irving, Austrians must remember that he had to assume a very high position without having had the training and culture that can be given only by a great national theatre with a highly trained audience and an established artistic tradition. . . . A theatre without a living drama is in the long run impossible; and when Irving had exhausted the old plays in which his personality was effective, he was—to be quite frank —too ignorant and old-fashioned to know how to choose fresh material. His greatest achievement was his social achievement, the redemption of his profession from Bohemianism, the imposing himself on the nation as one of the most eminent men in it, and the official acknowledgement of that estimate by the accolade. (*Pen Portraits*, pp. 161-65)

Shaw's appraisals of the actors and the managers, like his criticisms of the plays, should be understood in the light of his general program for the theater of his day. Whatever amounted to a repudiation of the obsolete and heralded the twentieth century met with his approval, while hangers-on from a bygone age displeased and, in gross cases, infuriated him. The wasting of talent struck him as virtually a crime and he urged, with all the rhetorical flourishes at his disposal, dramatists like Henry Arthur Jones and actors like Henry Irving and Ellen Terry to refuse to busy themselves with the mediocre and the old-fashioned and to use their creativity to embody a drama truly representative of the age in which they lived. Unfortunately, his hopes were largely unrealized, for there were not many Granville Barkers or Court Theatres during Shaw's lifetime to bolster his spirits.

Chapter 8

THE THEATER

IN READING the Shaw reviews or, for that matter, the reviews of any critic of the arts who is not merely a hack, we must keep in mind that the reviewer's standards of judgment are for the most part not the standards of the majority of people who attend the theater or the concert hall. As we have seen, Shaw thought of the theater as a temple—not figuratively, but actually. It was a place where a man's highest instincts could and should be nourished. Far from being a sour-faced Cato, however, Shaw could laugh with the best. And that wit and serious purpose are not at odds is demonstrated by most of his own plays. Since what he could do himself he seems to have expected of others, he believed that a few hours spent in the theater were simply not worth the trouble unless some sort of lasting stimulation were provided. For if the experience of going to the theater offers nothing more than a three-hour gambol, why is it to be preferred, say, to a couple of rounds of volley ball? Especially, one should add, when volley balls are so much more accessible—and cheap. Thus, after seeing a play of little value, Shaw commented: "But as a play, involving the effort of making up one's mind to go to the theatre, booking one's seat, going out at night, and so on—no, thank you" (II, 224). And after seeing two trifling entertainments he remarks that if the price of tickets were very low, perhaps seeing these plays would be a not unreasonable way of using up an evening. But at the current prices, "The playgoer who misses them will miss nothing but an evening's amusement" (II, 49).

A play must be quite good indeed to make it worth the trouble and expense of coming out to the theater: "The theatrical managers will not recognize that they have to compete with the British fireside, the slippers, the easy chair, the circulating library, and the illustrated press."[1] Theaters are traditionally uncomfortable, and though fanatic devotees of plays and operas endure almost any torture to attend, most other people, once the movies came into existence, would prefer a plush movie house to an expensive and uncomfortable theater. This is perhaps one of the reasons why the movies were to usurp the popular theater audience.

In 1888, after attending an opera at Covent Garden, Shaw wrote a bumptious letter to the manager, complaining about the hardships one had to endure to attend a performance:

I complain, to begin with, of Mr Augustus Harris taking upon himself to dictate to me what sort of coat I shall wear in a public theatre, merely because he happens to be the manager of that theatre. Next season, I shall purchase a stall for the most important evening I can select. I shall dress in white flannels. I shall then hire for the evening the most repulsive waiter I can find in the lowest oyster shop in London. I shall rub him with bacon crackling, smooth his hair with fried sausages, shower stale gravy upon him, season him with

Worcester sauce, and give him just enough drink to make him self assertive without making him actually drunk. With him I shall present myself at the stalls; explain that he is my brother; and that we have arranged that I am to see the opera unless evening dress is indispensable, in which case my brother, being in evening dress, must take my place. If other gentlemen will public spiritedly follow my example, the result is certain. The impertinent sumptuary regulation will disappear from the bills.[2]

Before the movies came into existence, the theater was attended by intense devotees and by people who wanted a pleasant enough evening on the town. But as for the people in between, "We have no theatre for quite ordinary cultivated people" (II, 214). In an essay on William Morris as an actor and dramatist, Shaw discusses the fact that Morris never went to the theater. "We have no theatre for men like William Morris" (II, 213-14). Furthermore, Shaw observes that many groups of people associated with the arts do not go to the theater—they go to concerts, they read. But

nobody goes to the theatre except the people who also go to Madame Tussaud's. Nobody writes for it, unless he is hopelessly stage struck and cannot help himself. It has no share in the leadership of thought: it does not even reflect its current. It does not create beauty: it apes fashion. It does not produce personal skill: our actors and actresses, with the exception of a few persons with natural gifts and graces, mostly miscultivated or half cultivated, are simply the middle-class section of the residuum. The curt insult with which Matthew Arnold dismissed it from consideration found it and left it utterly defenceless. And yet you ask me why Morris did not go to the theatre. In the name of common sense, why should he have gone? (II, 214)

Even the Lyceum's pretense of doing Shakespeare was too thin for a man of cultivation to be taken in by it. The theaters, then, were of little service either to the new or the old drama, the result being inevitable discouragement of serious dramatic composition. Shaw attributes much—perhaps most—of the blame for the enfeeblement of the modern theater to the actor-manager system:

We all know by this time that the effect of the actor-manager system is to impose on every dramatic author who wishes to have his work produced in first-rate style, the condition that there shall be a good part for the actor-manager in it. This is not in the least due to the vanity and jealousy of the actor-manager: it is due to his popularity. The strongest fascination at a theatre is the fascination of the actor or actress, not of the author. More people go to the Lyceum Theatre to see Mr Irving and Miss Ellen Terry than to see Shakespear's plays; at all events, it is certain that if Mr Irving were to present himself in as mutilated a condition as he presented King Lear, a shriek of horror would go up from all London.[3]

Shaw goes on to complain that as the number of actor-managers increases, it becomes harder and harder to assemble first-rate casts of actors, because there are not enough good actors to go around. As long as the production of plays is a business proposition rather than an artistic one, good casts cannot be assembled, for some of the best actors will be working for one actor-manager, some for another.

Furthermore, the actor-managers do not like to play Ibsen, because the Ibsen protagonists are very often not heroes, but scoundrels: "Man clings to the old pose, the old cheap heroism; and the actor in particular, whose life aspiration it has been to embody that pose, feels, with inexpressible misgiving, the earth crumbling beneath his feet as the enthusiasm his heroism once excited turns to pity and ridicule."[4] And, naturally, the leading ladies who are attached to the actor-managers must forfeit *their* chance to play a fascinating modern woman if the manager refuses to do an "advanced" play. (Shaw always has Ellen Terry in mind when he makes such statements as these.)

In *Love Among the Artists*, where so many of Shaw's views on art make an early appearance, there is a delightful scene in which an actor-manager is described as he trains his actors, among whom is Madge Brailsford, a major character in the novel. "He was a 'star,' recognizing no part and no influence but his own. She and her colleagues were dwarfed and put out of countenance; their scenes were cut short and hurried through. . . . Naturally, they all hated Shakespeare; and the audiences distinctly preferring the tragedian to the poet, never protested against his palming off on them versions by Cibber or Garrick as genuine Shakespearean plays."[5]

Somewhat jokingly Shaw suggests that we are now ripe for the emergence of the actress-manageress—and the collapse of the managerial system altogether: "I don't think the actress-manageress is going to do much good, because, obviously, she will want plays with good parts for the woman and bad parts for the men; and so, though we shall have two sorts of bad plays instead of one—the actress-manageress's play at half the theatres and the actor-manager's play at the other half, we shall be as far as ever from the genuine drama."[6] After all is said and done, it is business and its exigencies which must take a good deal of the blame for the ill-success of the drama, concludes Shaw. And this, of course, is one of the perennial problems in all the arts. The serious dramatist is willing to write his plays for the benefit of a small, select audience, with a mere pittance as his compensation. But the theater cannot afford such magnanimity. In order to remain open, the theaters must take in a fairly large amount of money. To do this, they must present plays or actors that will draw large numbers of people to attend. As a result, the *avant garde* works are not played.

One of Shaw's hopes was the suburban theater. To begin with, he believed that theaters, like churches, should be sprinkled throughout a city and its environs and not be confined to the congested downtown areas. The obstacles to be overcome in attending a theater, especially when it is far from one's home, are discouraging and one is apt to be content to stay home near the fireside. With theaters within convenient distance, people should be more willing to bother to spend an evening attending a play. As the suburban theaters increased, to Shaw's approval, he found that they could perform mediocre London successes virtually as well as the fashionable West End theaters. This seemed a hopeful sign, for if the audiences at London successes were to decrease because the local theaters could do as well and offered the additional advantages of proximity and lower prices, perhaps these fashionable West End theaters would be induced to exhibit better plays, possibly at more reasonable prices. However, this was to come about mainly through the Vedrenne-Barker empire at the Court Theater, starting in 1904. Here, the plays of Shaw were produced abundantly and pre-eminently, and although a high point was reached in the

English theater, no lasting movement towards the realization of Shaw's ideal was inaugurated.

There were, however, a number of small-scale theatrical groups which served the cause of art during the nineties somewhat the way the off-Broadway theaters are serving it at the present time. One of these, the Elizabethan Stage Society, was devoted to the performance of earlier plays in appropriately stark settings, such as inn yards. With their limited budget, their limited costumes, and their limited theater, they had little to do but pay attention to Shakespeare's words, or Marlowe's words, with the hardly surprising result that Shaw regarded their performances of English classics as altogether superior to the Lyceum frolics based on Shakespeare.

The Elizabethan Stage Society was principally the creation of William Poel. Although formally established in 1894, the Society produced *Measure for Measure* in 1893 at the Royalty Theatre, which was converted to resemble an Elizabethan playhouse. This was followed in 1894 by *Twelfth Night*. Although Poel tampered with and bowdlerized his Elizabethan texts, his productions contrasted favorably with the standard Lyceum type of Shakespearean production, which made no attempt at authenticity. Shaw, as we have already seen, was pleased by the incantatory quality of the recitation of Poel's "unknown" actors.[7]

The most substantial of these experimental theater groups was the Independent Theatre, organized by J. T. Grein in 1891, whose aim was to give performances of plays of artistic merit which the commercial theaters would not wish to handle:[8]

He accordingly hired a cheap public hall in Tottenham Court Road, and, though his resources fell far short of those with which an ambitious young professional man ventures upon giving a dance, made a bold start by announcing a performance of Ghosts to inaugurate "The Independent Theatre" on the lines of the Théâtre Libre of Paris. The result was that he received sufficient support both in money and gratuitous professional aid to enable him to give the performance at the Royalty Theatre; and throughout the following week he shared with Ibsen the distinction of being abusively discussed to an extent that must have amply convinced him that his efforts had not passed unheeded.[9]

One of the motives of the Independent Theatre was to overcome the obstacle to the production of adult drama which was posed by the Examiner of Plays. Inspired by the Shelley Society's presentation in 1886 of *The Cenci*, banned by the Examiner, the Independent Theatre used the device of the private subscription. When the Examiner refused to allow a public performance of *Ghosts*, the Independent Theatre was founded, and it produced the play in 1891. Its prospectus contained, besides an announcement of *Ghosts*, a list of plays by Ibsen, Lessing, Strindberg, and other forward-looking dramatists, although not all of the announced plays were ultimately produced. Only "invited guests" were permitted to attend, since performances open to the general public were subject to the Examiner's approval. Grein invited so many friends that trouble developed in finding a suitably large theater, a problem which was not helped by the public opposition voiced by the press. However, the Royalty Theatre was obtained for one performance. So many people wanted to attend that a rehearsal was done for the overflow subscribers two nights before the actual performance.

Interestingly, the Independent Theatre also performed Shaw's first play, *Widowers' Houses*, in 1892.[10]

In 1907, J. T. Grein looked back upon the early days of the Society he had founded, recalling his production of Jones and Pinero in Holland in 1890:

So great was the success of these English plays at Amsterdam that the managers of the Royal Subsidized Theatre sent me a cheque for fifty pounds to be used in the interest of art in England. At the same time I had received another cheque for thirty pounds for the translation of an English play. With these gigantic sums, in the wake of Antoine of Paris, I founded the Independent Theatre, the first performance of which elicited no less than five hundred articles, mostly vituperating Ibsen, whose 'Ghosts' inaugurated the movement, and obtained for me the honorary, if somewhat unflattering title of 'the best abused man in London.' In parenthesis, I should add here that the distinction clung to me for many years, that some families closed their doors against me because I had produced an immoral play, and that a well-known journalist, since dead, refused to be present at a banquet if I were invited. It cost me practically ten years of my life to overcome the prejudice created by an undertaking which even the enemy must admit has left its mark upon the history of our stage.[11]

The Society, however, lasted only six years. Another group, the New Century Theatre, was established later in the nineties by William Archer, H. W. Massingham, Alfred Sutro, and Elizabeth Robins. Their motives were similar to Grein's but their organization less firm, for Shaw points out in his review of April 10, 1897, that this new group was nothing more than a new name for the occasional matinees of good plays which Elizabeth Robins had been giving for years. The only solution to the problem of obtaining stagings for first-rate new plays, reiterates Shaw, is the establishment of a national theater in the fashion of the festival playhouse at Bayreuth, a theater in continuous existence physically, organizationally, and repertorially, an achievement which none of the new *avant garde* drama groups could boast.

An indispensable part of the theater and the drama is the audience. It is unfortunate, however, that for the most part, an audience will prefer nothing to something. And the audience dictates commercial success. Shaw's classic statement of the relation of audience to author occurs in his fairly well-known review of Henry James's *Guy Domville*, which might be described as a delicate flop:

The truth about Mr James's play is no worse than that it is out of fashion. Any dramatically disposed young gentleman who, cultivating sentiment on a little alcohol, and gaining an insight into the mysteries of the eternal feminine by a couple of squalid intrigues, meanwhile keeps well aloof from art and philosophy, and thus preserves his innocence of the higher life of the senses and of the intellect, can patch up a play tomorrow which will pass as real drama with the gentlemen who deny that distinction to the works of Mr Henry James. No doubt, if the literary world were as completely dominated by the admirers of Mr Rider Haggard as the dramatic world is by their first cousins, we should be told that Mr James cannot write a novel. That is not criticism: it is a mere begging of the question. There is no reason why life as we find it in Mr James's novels—life, that is, in which passion is subordinate to intellect and to fastidious artistic taste— should not be represented on the stage. If it is real to

Mr James, it must be real to others; and why should not these others have their drama instead of being banished from the theatre (to the theatre's great loss) by the monotony and vulgarity of drama in which passion is everything, intellect nothing, and art only brought in by the incidental outrages upon it. As it happens, I am not myself in Mr James's camp: in all the life that has energy enough to be interesting to me, subjective volition, passion, will, make intellect the merest tool. But there is in the centre of that cyclone a certain calm spot where cultivated ladies and gentlemen live on independent incomes or by pleasant artistic occupations. It is there that Mr James's art touches life, selecting whatever is graceful, exquisite, or dignified in its serenity. It is not life as imagined by the pit or gallery, or even by the stalls: it is, let us say, the ideal of the balcony; but that is no reason why the pit and gallery should excommunicate it on the ground that it has no blood and entrails in it, and have its sentence formulated for it by the fiercely ambitious and wilful professional man in the stalls. The whole case against its adequacy really rests on its violation of the cardinal stage convention that love is the most irresistible of all the passions. Since most people go to the theatre to escape from reality, this convention is naturally dear to a world in which love, all powerful in the secret, unreal, day-dreaming life of the imagination, is in the real active life the abject slave of every trifling habit, prejudice, and cowardice, easily stifled by shyness, class feeling, and pecuniary prudence, or diverted from what is theatrically assumed to be its hurricane course by such obstacles as a thick ankle, a cockney accent, or an unfashionable hat. In the face of this, is it good sense to accuse Mr Henry James of a want of grip of the realities of life because he gives us a hero who sacrifices his love to a strong and noble vocation for the Church?

213

And yet when some unmannerly playgoer, untouched by either love or religion, chooses to send a derisive howl from the gallery at such a situation, we are to sorrowfully admit, if you please, that Mr James is no dramatist, on the general ground that "the drama's laws the drama's patrons give." Pray, which of its patrons? —the cultivated majority who, like myself and all the ablest of my colleagues, applauded Mr James on Saturday, or the handful of rowdies who brawled at him? It is the business of the dramatic critic to educate these dunces, not to echo them. (I, 6-7)

This fine piece of Shavian criticism, Shaw's second review for the *Saturday Review*, perhaps implies that more people appreciated James's play than was actually the case. Certainly even many of the dramatic critics who saw it reacted unfavorably, though perhaps they were not among the "ablest of my colleagues" whom Shaw refers to.

In the course of his reviews, Shaw observes that there are slight but clear evidences of the refinement of taste among the theatergoing public. He contrasts the crudeness of some of the plays of the sixties, seventies, and eighties with a few of the best modern plays, not to mention those of Ibsen, as evidence. Surely the Victorian theater had a difficult time trying to recover from the disastrous effects of what Rowell calls "The New Drama"—that is, the drama of the early nineteenth century.[12] By the time Shaw began to review, Pinero was emerging from his more primitive period, and the Lyceum had at least added a superficial refinement to the physical elements of the theater. But there was still much to lament, such as the rowdy behavior of the inhabitants of cheap seats. Shaw recommends that other dramatic critics vigorously protest the outbreaks of rowdies in the gallery. No doubt most of the audience were well behaved, but "they should not allow the minority to discredit them by insulting every actress whose part requires her to make some demonstration of affection to her stage lover" (II, 208). There is a very long tirade against the gallery in the review of March 6, 1897. Apparently, people who disliked a play began to hiss and boo the applauding people who liked the play, until a frenzied uproar was the result. An additional incentive for uproar was the customary appearance of the author of the play on the first night. The problem became so great in Shaw's day that police had to be summoned. Shaw concludes:

What possibility is there of fine art flourishing where full licence to yell—the licence of the cockpit and prize-ring—is insisted on by men who never dream of misbehaving themselves elsewhere?

If I were starting in theatrical management tomorrow, I should probably abolish the shilling gallery on first nights, and make the lowest price of admission either half a crown or threepence, according to the district. . . . Shouting can convey nothing but "Booh!" or "Hooray!" except, as I have said, in moments of real enthusiasm, quite foreign to the demonstrativeness of our theatre fanciers and greenroom gossip swallowers. Best of all would be no applause; but that will come later on. For the present, since we cannot contain ourselves wholly, let us at least express ourselves humanly and sensibly. (III, 69)

The most interesting of Shaw's pronouncements on the behavior of the audience occurred in a leaflet supplied at the Kingsway Theatre in 1913 at performances of *John Bull's Other Island:*

Dear Sir or Madam,
    It is your custom to receive my plays with the most

215

generous and unrestrained applause. You sometimes compel the performers to pause at the end of every line until your laughter has quieted down. I am not ungrateful, but may I ask you a few questions? . . .

Do you not think that the naturalness of the representation must be destroyed, and therefore your own pleasure greatly diminished, when the audience insists on taking part in it by shouts of applause and laughter, and the actors have repeatedly to stop acting until the noise is over[?] . . .

Can you not imagine how a play which has been rehearsed to perfection in dead silence without an audience must be upset, disjointed, and spun out to a wearisome length by an audience which refuses to enjoy it silently?

Have you noticed that if you laugh loudly and repeatedly for two hours, you get tired and cross, and are sorry next morning that you did not stay at home? . . .

Would you dream of stopping the performance of a piece of music to applaud every bar that happened to please you? and do you not know that an act of a play is intended, just like a piece of music, to be heard without interruption from beginning to end?[13]

All things considered, Shaw manifested remarkable forbearance throughout his entire career. He had great patience too. For unlike the alienated artists of the twentieth century, whose audiences must train themselves, Shaw, as critic and as artist, had an evangelical personality which—whatever scorn it may have had for the rabble—could not achieve its goals without actively seeking to lure and develop its audience. This Zarathustrian combination of philosophic aloofness and condescension to educate is what Eric Bentley has aptly referred to as "the fool in Christ."

45. *The Dramatic Theory of George Bernard Shaw*, University of Nebraska Ph.D. Dissertation, 1962, pp. 103-04.
46. Shaw, "The Religion of the Pianoforte," *Fortnightly Review*, LV (n.s.), 264. Also in *How to Become a Musical Critic*, ed. Dan H. Laurence, London, 1960.
47. *Shaw on Theatre*, p. 151.
48. "Pianoforte," pp. 263-64.
49. *Ibid.*, pp. 260-61.
50. *Shaw on Theatre*, p. 185.
51. *Ibid.*, p. 229.
52. Shaw, p. 191.
53. London, 1896, pp. 63, 66.
54. *Letters*, p. 318.
55. *Bernard Shaw*, pp. 193-94, 198-99.

Chapter 3: Nineteenth-Century Drama

1. *Letters*, p. 126.
2. George Rowell, *The Victorian Theatre*, London, 1956, p. 31.
3. *Renascence of the English Drama*, London, 1895, p. 11.
4. *Shaw and the Nineteenth-Century Theater*, Princeton, 1963, p. 38.
5. Rowell, p. 80.
6. *Ibid.*, p. 81.
7. See *Camille and Other Plays*, ed. Stephen S. Stanton, New York, 1957, preface. See also Elmer N. Engstrom, "Shaw and the Well Made Play," Columbia University Master's Thesis, 1948 (not microfilmed). See also Stephen S. Stanton's *English Drama and the French Well-Made Play*, Columbia University Ph.D. Dissertation, 1955, introductory chapter, *passim*.
8. Stanton, *Camille*, p. vii, n.
9. Engstrom, p. 1.
10. Stanton, *Camille*, p. xxxix.
11. *The Old Drama and the New*, New York, 1926, pp. 253-54.
12. *Shaw on Theatre*, p. 220.
13. *Ibid.*, p. 133.
14. *The Theatrical 'World' of 1897*, London, 1898, pp. 196-97.
15. Based on Rowell; also A. Nicoll, *A History of English Drama, 1660-1900*, V, Cambridge, 1959.

16. *Advice to a Young Critic,* p. 23.

17. *Ibid.,* p. 22.

18. *Letters,* p. 501.

19. *Ibid.,* p. 402.

20. *The Theatrical 'World' of 1895,* London, 1896, Review of *The Notorious Mrs. Ebbsmith.*

21. *The Old Drama and the New,* p. 310.

22. *George Bernard Shaw: Playboy and Prophet,* New York, 1932, p. 341.

23. Nicoll, pp. 163-64.

24. Nicoll, p. 170.

25. *Renasence,* pp. 166-67.

26. *Shaw on Theatre,* pp. 220-21.

27. *Ibid.,* p. 268.

28. Stanton, *Camille,* pp. ix, x; Meisel, *passim.*

CHAPTER 4: Shakespeare and Elizabethan Drama

1. Additional illustrations of points I raise in this chapter can be found in *Shaw on Shakespeare.*

2. There is a discussion of the externality of much of the motivation of Shakespeare's characters in Albert H. Silverman, "Bernard Shaw's Shakespeare Criticism," *PMLA,* LXXII, 722-36.

3. *George Bernard Shaw,* New York, 1956, p. 78.

4. Sylvan Barnet, "Bernard Shaw on Tragedy," *PMLA,* LXXI, 891.

5. J. P. Smith, "Superman versus Man: Bernard Shaw on Shakespeare," *Yale Review,* XLII, 75-76.

6. See Barnet; also Eric Bentley, *The Playwright as Thinker,* New York, 1946, p. 142.

7. S. C. Sen Gupta, *The Art of Bernard Shaw,* Oxford, 1936, pp. 231-32. See also Silverman, pp. 722-28.

8. Campbell *Letters,* p. 248.

9. *Shaw on Theatre,* p. 221.

10. *Ibid.,* pp. 159-62.

11. *Ibid.,* pp. 167-68.

12. *Ibid.,* p. 96.

13. In the Preface to the fourth edition of *The Perfect Wagnerite* Shaw wrote: "One had to admit at Bayreuth that here was the utmost perfection of the pictorial stage, and that its machinery could go no further. Nevertheless, having seen it at its best, fresh from Wagner's own influence, I must also admit that my favorite way of enjoying a performance of The

Ring is to sit at the back of a box, comfortable on two chairs, feet up, and listen without looking. The truth is, a man whose imagination cannot serve him better than the most costly devices of the imitative scenepainter, should not go to the theatre, and as a matter of fact does not. In planning his Bayreuth theatre, Wagner was elaborating what he had better have scrapped altogether" (*Essays*, p. 155).

CHAPTER 5: Ibsen

1. Based on Miriam Franc, *Ibsen in England*, Chaps. I, II, and p. 76.
2. *Shaw on Theatre*, p. 1.
3. "Bernard Shaw at Eighty," in *Critical Survey*, ed. Kronenberger.
4. Franc, p. 35.
5. Sen Gupta, p. 239.
6. Raymond Williams, *Drama from Ibsen to Eliot*, London, 1952, p. 66, n. 3.
7. Gassner, "Shaw on Ibsen and the Drama of Ideas," in *Ideas in the Drama* [7], New York and London, 1964; Gerould, "George Bernard Shaw's Criticism of Ibsen," *Comparative Literature*, XV, No. 1, 130-45.
8. Gerould, p. 138.
9. Gassner, p. 73.
10. Gerould, p. 141.
11. Gassner, p. 72.
12. Franc, p. 36.

CHAPTER 6: The Censorship

1. Watson Nicholson, *The Struggle For a Free Stage in London*, Boston, 1906, pp. 48-49.
2. *Shaw on Theatre*, pp. 74-75.
3. *Letters*, p. 489.
4. Quoted by R. M. Smith in *Modern Dramatic Censorship: George Bernard Shaw*, Indiana University Doctoral Dissertation, 1953, p. 11.
5. *Shaw on Theatre*, p. 70.
6. *Ibid.*, p. 173.
7. Mander and Mitchenson, p. 31.
8. *Shaw on Theatre*, p. 251. Shaw discusses this matter at great length in his speech, "Censorship as a Police Duty," in *Platform and Pulpit*.

9. *Ibid.*, pp. 78-79.

10. *Ibid.*, pp. 79-80. Since this chapter was completed, an article in the New York *Times*, June 22, 1967, states that recent activity in Parliament virtually assures the abolition of the censorship of the drama in the near future.

11. Smith, pp. 104, 160.

CHAPTER 7: Actors and Acting

1. Rowell, Chapter 1.

2. *George Bernard Shaw*, p. 48.

3. *Florence Farr, Bernard Shaw, W. B. Yeats*, ed. Cliford Bax, New York, 1942, pp. 7-8.

4. *Ibid.*, pp. 20-23.

5. Campbell Letters, pp. 305-06.

6. *Advice to a Young Critic*, p. 122.

7. Mander and Mitchenson, p. 63.

8. London, 1950, p. 101.

9. *Letters*, p. 492.

10. *Platform and Pulpit*, pp. 12-23.

11. *Shaw on Theatre*, p. 154.

12. *Ibid.*, p. 153.

13. *Ibid.*, pp. 153-59.

14. *Ibid.*, pp. 279-89.

15. *Ibid.*, p. 281.

16. *Ibid.*, p. 283.

17. *Ibid.*, p. 284.

18. *Ibid.*, p. 287.

19. *Ibid.*, p. 275. (See pp. 270-72 for more details on Sullivan.)

20. *Ibid.*, pp. 274-75.

21. *Ibid.*, p. 278. With Shaw's recollection of Sullivan so enthusiastic, it is not surprising that Allardyce Nicoll should receive a reprimand for failing to give Sullivan any mention at all—at least in the edition of Nicoll's *History of English Drama* that Shaw read. However, the most recent edition includes a reference to Sullivan in a footnote.

22. *Letters*, p. 521.

23. *Ibid.*, p. 524.

24. *Ibid.*, p. 499.

25. Mander and Mitchenson, p. 160.

26. *Letters*, pp. 215-16.

27. *Ibid.*, p. 337.

28. *Ibid.*, p. 478.

29. *Ibid.*, p. 502.
30. *Ibid.*, p. 506.
31. *Ibid.*, pp. 765-66.
32. Terry *Letters*, p. xx. An interesting sidelight on this impression (which was regarded as unfair by Laurence Irving in his book *Sir Henry Irving*) is to be found in Rattray's *Bernard Shaw: A Chronicle*. In a footnote we are given another eminent writer's impression of Irving—that of Henry James: "His voice is apparently wholly unavailable for purposes of declamation. To say that he speaks badly is to go too far; to my sense he simply does not speak at all—in any way that, in an actor, can be called speaking. Shakespeare's finest lines pass from his lips without his paying the scantiest tribute to their quality. Of what the French call *diction*—of the art of delivery—he has apparently not a suspicion. This forms three-fourths of an actor's obligation, and in Mr. Irving's acting these three-fourths are simply cancelled" (Rattray, p. 128 n.1).
33. Terry *Letters*, p. xxv.
34. *Ibid.*, p. xx.
35. *Ibid.*, pp. xxii-xxiii.
36. *Ibid.*, p. xxiv.
37. *Ibid.*, pp. 306-07. (See the Preface to the Terry Letters for a lengthy discussion of Irving.)
38. *Letters*, p. 751.
39. *Ibid.*, p. 752.

Chapter 8: The Theater

1. *Shaw on Theatre*, p. 47.
2. *Letters*, p. 191.
3. *Shaw on Theatre*, pp. 44-45.
4. *Ibid.*, p. 50.
5. P. 114.
6. *Advice to a Young Critic*, p. 39.
7. Based on Robert Speaight, *William Poel and the Elizabethan Revival*, London, 1954.
8. Shaw describes Grein's achievement in an Appendix to *The Quintessence of Ibsenism* of 1891, the first edition. The Appendix has not subsequently been included but can be found in *Shaw on Theatre*.
9. *Shaw on Theatre*, p. 10.
10. Based on Chapters 4 and 5 of Michael Orme, *J. T. Grein: The Story of a Pioneer*, London, 1936.

11. Quoted by Miriam Franc, pp. 86-87.
12. See Chapter 3: Nineteenth-Century Drama, above.
13. Mander and Mitchenson, p. 96.

Bibliography

I. Works by Shaw:

Advice to a Young Critic, ed. E. J. West. New York, Crown Publishers, 1955.

Bernard Shaw and Mrs. Patrick Campbell: Their Correspondence, ed. Alan Dent. New York, Alfred A. Knopf, 1952.

Bernard Shaw's Letters to Granville Barker, ed. C. B. Purdom. New York, Theatre Arts Books, 1957.

Collected Letters, 1874-1897, ed. Dan H. Laurence. London, Max Reinhardt, 1965.

Complete Plays of Bernard Shaw, The. London, Odhams Press, n.d. (1950's ?).

Dramatic Opinions and Essays, ed. James Huneker. 2 vols. New York, Brentano's, 1909.

Ellen Terry and Bernard Shaw: A Correspondence, ed. Christopher St. John. New York, G. Putnam's Sons, 1931.

Florence Farr, Bernard Shaw, W. B. Yeats, ed. Clifford Bax. New York, Dodd, Mead and Company, 1942.

How to Become a Musical Critic, ed. Dan H. Laurence. New York, Hill and Wang, 1960.

London Music in 1888-89. London, Constable and Company, 1950.

Love Among the Artists. London, Constable and Company, 1950.

Major Critical Essays. London, Constable and Company, 1955.

Music in London, 1890-94. 3 vols. London, Constable and Company, 1956.

Our Theatres in the Nineties. 3 vols. London, Constable and Company, 1948.

Pen Portraits and Reviews. London, Constable and Company, 1949.

Platform and Pulpit, ed. Dan H. Laurence. New York, Hill and Wang, 1961.

Prefaces by Bernard Shaw. London, Odhams Press Ltd., 1938.

"Religion of the Pianoforte, The," *Fortnightly Review,* LV(n.s.), 254-66.

Religious Speeches of Bernard Shaw, ed. Warren S. Smith. University Park, The Pennsylvania State University Press, 1963.

Shaw on Shakespeare, ed. Edwin Wilson. New York, E. P. Dutton and Company, Inc., 1961.

Shaw on Theatre, ed. E. J. West. New York, Hill and Wang, 1958.

Sixteen Self-Sketches. New York, Dodd, Mead and Company, 1949.

To a Young Actress, ed. Peter Tomkins. New York, Clarkson N. Potter, 1960.

II. Other works:

Archer, William. *The Old Drama and the New.* New York, Dodd, Mead and Company, 1926.

———. *The Theatrical 'World' of 1895.* London, Walter Scott, Ltd., 1896.

———. *The Theatrical 'World' of 1896.* London, Walter Scott, Ltd., 1897.

———. *The Theatrical 'World of 1897.* London, Walter Scott, Ltd., 1898.

Barnet, Sylvan. "Bernard Shaw on Tragedy," *PMLA,* LXXI, 888-99.

Bennett, Kenneth C. *George Bernard Shaw's Philosophy of Art.* Indiana University Doctoral Dissertation, 1961.

Bentley, Eric. *Bernard Shaw.* Norfolk, Conn., New Directions Books, 1957.

———. *The Playwright as Thinker.* New York, Reynal and Hitchcock, 1946.

Bernd, Daniel Walter. *The Dramatic Theory of George Bernard Shaw.* University of Nebraska Doctoral Dissertation, 1962.

Boynton, H. W. "Shaw as Critic," *Atlantic Monthly,* XCIX, 553-60.

Camille and Other Plays, ed. Stephen S. Stanton. New York, Hill and Wang, 1957.

Chesterton, G. K. *George Bernard Shaw*. New York, Hill and Wang, 1956.

Du Cann, G. C. L. *The Loves of G.B.S.* New York, Funk and Wagnalls Co. Inc., 1963.

Dunbar, Janet. *Mrs. G.B.S.* London, George G. Harrap and Co., Ltd., 1963.

English Dramatic Critics, The, ed. James Agate. New York, Hill and Wang, n.d. (1960 ?).

Emerson, Flora Elizabeth. *English Dramatic Critics of the Nineties*. Bryn Mawr College Doctoral Dissertation, 1953.

Engstrom, Elmer N. *Bernard Shaw and the Well Made Play*. Columbia University Master's Thesis, 1948.

Ervine, St. John Greer. *Bernard Shaw: His Life, Work, and Friends*. London, Constable and Company, 1956.

Franc, Miriam A. *Ibsen in England*. Boston, The Four Seas Company, 1919.

Gassner, John. "Shaw on Ibsen and the Drama of Ideas," *Ideas in the Drama* [7], New York and London, Columbia University Press, 1964, pp. 71-100.

G. B. Shaw, A Collection of Critical Essays, ed. R. J. Kaufmann. Englewood Cliffs, N.J., Prentice-Hall, Inc., 1965.

George Bernard Shaw: A Critical Survey, ed. Louis Kronenberger. Cleveland and New York, The World Publishing Co., 1953.

Gerould, Daniel Charles. "George Bernard Shaw's Criticism of Ibsen," *Comparative Literature*, XV, No. 1, 130-45.

Glicksberg, C. I. "The Criticism of Bernard Shaw," *South Atlantic Quarterly*, L, 96-108.

Hankin, St. J. "Bernard Shaw as a Critic," *Fortnightly Review*, LXXXVII, 1057-68.

Harris, Frank. *Bernard Shaw*. New York, Simon and Schuster, 1931.

Henderson, Archibald. *George Bernard Shaw: Man of the Century*. New York, Appleton-Century-Crofts, Inc., 1956.

―――. *George Bernard Shaw, Playboy and Prophet*. New York, Appleton, 1932.

―――. *Table Talk of G.B.S.* New York and London, Harper and Brothers, 1925.

Irvine, William. *The Universe of G.B.S.* New York, Whittlesey House, McGraw-Hill, 1949.

Joad,, C. E. M. *Shaw.* London, Victor Gollancz Ltd., 1949.

Jones, Henry Arthur. *Renascence of the English Drama.* London, Macmillan and Company, 1895.

Kaye, Julian B. *Bernard Shaw and the Nineteenth-Century Tradition.* Norman, University of Oklahoma Press, 1958.

Langner, Lawrence. *G.B.S. and the Lunatic.* New York, Atheneum, 1963.

Mander, R., and J. Mitchenson. *Theatrical Companion to Shaw.* London, Rockliff Publishing Corp., 1954.

Meisel, Martin. *Shaw and the Nineteenth-Century Theater.* Princeton, Princeton University Press, 1963.

Nethercot, Arthur H. *The First Five Lives of Annie Besant.* Chicago, University of Chicago Press, 1960.

———. *Men and Supermen: The Shavian Portrait Gallery.* Cambridge, Harvard University Press, 1954.

Nicholson, Watson. *The Struggle for a Free Stage in London.* New York and Boston, Houghton Mifflin, 1906.

Nicoll, Allardyce. *A History of Late Nineteenth Century Drama: 1850-1900.* 2 vols. Cambridge, Cambridge University Press, 1959.

Nineteenth Century Plays, ed. George Rowell. Oxford, Oxford University Press, 1956.

Ohmann, Richard. *Shaw: The Style and the Man.* Middletown, Conn., Wesleyan University Press, 1962.

Orme, Michael (Mrs. Alice Augusta Grein). *J. T. Grein: The Story of a Pioneer.* London, J. D. Murray, 1936.

Pearson, Hesketh. *G.B.S. A Full Length Portrait.* New York and London, Harper and Brothers, 1942.

———. *G.B.S. A Postscript.* New York, Harper and Brothers, 1950.

Rattray, R. F. *Bernard Shaw: A Chronicle.* Luton, Leagrave Press, Ltd., 1951.

Rosset, Benjamin C. *Shaw of Dublin, The Formative Years.* University Park, The Pennsylvania State University Press, 1964.

Rowell, George. *The Victorian Theatre.* London, Oxford University Press, 1956.

Sen Gupta, S. C. *The Art of Bernard Shaw.* London and New York, Oxford University Press, 1936.

Shavian, The. London, Shaw Society, 45 Steeplestone Close.

Shaw Bulletin (becomes *Shaw Review*). Shaw Society of America, Inc., The Pennsylvania State University Press.

Silverman, Albert H. "Bernard Shaw's Shakespeare Criticism," *PMLA*, LXXII, 722-36.

Smith, J. P. "Superman vs. Man: Bernard Shaw on Shakespeare," *Yale Review*, XLII, 75-76.

————. *The Unrepentant Pilgrim. A Study of the Development of Bernard Shaw.* Boston, Houghton Mifflin Co., 1965.

Smith, Robert McCaughan. *Modern Dramatic Censorship: George Bernard Shaw.* Indiana University Doctoral Dissertation, 1953.

Speaight, Robert. *William Poel and the Elizabethan Revival.* London, William Heinemann Ltd., 1954.

Stanton, Stephen S. *English Drama and the French Well-Made Play.* Columbia University Doctoral Dissertation, 1955.

————. "Shaw's Debt to Scribe," *PMLA*, LXXVI, 575-85.

Ward, A. C. *Bernard Shaw.* New York, Longmans, Green, 1952.

West, E. J. "G.B.S., Music and Shakespearean Blank Verse," *University of Colorado Studies*, Series B (Humanities), II, 344-56.

————. "G.B.S. on Shakespearean Production," *SP*, XLV, 216-35.

————. "Shaw's Criticism of Ibsen: A Reconsideration," *University of Colorado Studies*, Series in Language and Literature, No. 4, 101-27.

Williams, Raymond. *Drama from Ibsen to Eliot.* London, Chatto and Windus, 1952.

Williamson, Audrey. *Bernard Shaw: Man and Writer.* New York, The Crowell-Collier Press, 1963.

Winsten, Stephen. *G.B.S. 90.* New York, Dodd, Mead and Co., 1946.

Index